STAFF DEVELOPMENT:
The Key
to Effective
Gifted Education Programs

STAFF DEVELOPMENT:
The Key to Effective Gifted Education Programs

A Service Publication by the
Professional Development Division of the
National Association for Gifted Children

Co-Editors:

Peggy Dettmer, Ph.D.
Kansas State University

Mary Landrum, Ph.D.
Kent State University

Copy Editor:
Carolyn R. Cooper, Ph.D.
Baltimore School District

Graphics:

Norma Dyck
Kansas State University

Jane More Loeb
Shawnee Mission, Kansas,
School District

The National Association for Gifted Children
1707 L Street, NW, Suite 550
Washington, DC 20036
(202) 785-4268
http://www.nagc.org

A Service Publication of the
National Association for Gifted Children

©1998, National Association for Gifted Children
Cover image ©Photodisc Inc.

Cover design by Libby Lindsey

ISBN 1-882664-41-8

Prufrock Press • P.O. Box 8813 • Waco • Texas • 76714
(800) 998-2208 • FAX (800) 240-0333
http://www.prufrock.com • Prufrock@prufrock.com

Table of Contents

Foreword

from
The Professional Development Division
of the National Association for Gifted Children

This publication is created for and dedicated to every educator who, at one time or another, has:
- researched;
- participated in;
- planned;
- presented;
- hosted;
- evaluated; and/or
- followed through on

any inservice or staff development for educating gifted and talented students.

The National Association for Gifted Children (NAGC) provides this publication as a guide for gifted education program facilitators to plan, facilitate, and evaluate the inservice and staff development in their schools and their community settings. Any royalties from the publication are directed to the Professional Development Division of NAGC for promoting staff development. Many current and former participants in the Professional Development Division and its predecessor, the Inservice Training Committee on Gifted Education, have contributed to the ideas and materials within this book.

Background of Staff Development

Staff development is an integral part of teaching and learning. Facilitators for gifted programs must be able to plan, implement, and evaluate staff development experiences for a variety of school personnel and support role groups. Successful staff development experiences will increase interest in gifted education and commitment to gifted education. However, along with those opportunities will come responsibilities for managing such an important professional tool.

Too little attention has been directed toward developing the competencies that gifted education staff need in order to provide effective gifted program staff development for schools and communities. Not many textbooks and resource materials include more than a cursory overview of the subject, if they mention it at all. Few research studies exist in the gifted education literature that assess the impact staff development can have on teacher effectiveness with high ability students. Most gifted education personnel do conduct awareness sessions or workshops on particular strategies from time to time, but many have had little preparation and practice in staff development methodology.

Studies by Joyce and Showers (1988) indicate that all teachers can learn powerful and complex teaching strategies if they participate in well-designed staff development focusing on those strategies. This has important implications for gifted education personnel. Perceiving the learning needs of gifted students and understanding the curricular implications of those needs are vital for constructing the educational programming they require. Such perceptions and understandings can be cultivated with high-quality staff development.

It has been recognized for more than two decades that teachers do adopt more accepting and facilitative attitudes toward gifted students after just one course in the education of the gifted. However, general teacher education courses seldom address characteristics and needs of gifted learners beyond a perfunctory chapter or a one-shot lecture. So beginning teachers enter their classrooms ill-prepared to address the challenges created by gifted students and their curricular needs. Novice teachers have few opportunities to learn about gifted student needs from the day they complete their teacher preparation program to that very first day in their own classrooms where they can expect to have one or more gifted students. Then they become caught up in the daily pressures of coping with the general needs of all students and the special needs of students who find it hard to learn or unpleasant to be in school.

Many experienced teachers do develop strategies for teaching gifted over a number of years while they are on the job and engaging in a variety of school situations with their gifted students. A few educators learn about gifted students through courses in gifted education at universities and colleges. Some glean information and techniques from events such as the annual conference of the National Association for Gifted Children, or state and regional conferences. However, the vehicle most accessible to all and most promising for serving local needs is the staff development provided by the school district or cooperative.

Unfortunately, staff development—and one shot inservice sessions in particular—have been regarded by too many educators as irrelevant,

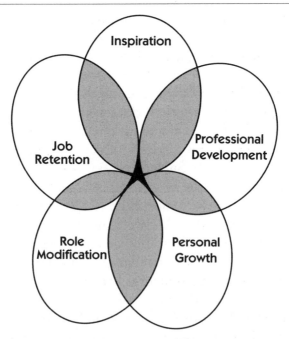

Figure 1: Purposes of Staff Development

time-wasteful, poorly presented, and lacking in follow-up assistance. Therefore, in order to utilize this powerful tool for understanding the needs of gifted individuals and planning for their education, gifted education personnel must develop excellent skills as staff developers.

Gifted education staff developers will need to aim toward a wide range of educators in a variety of roles. The gifted program staff development should target one or more of five key purposes that exist for any staff development activity: professional development in education of the gifted; personal growth as an educator and life-long learner; job retention with continued certification; role modification to function in other school structures; inspiration as a teacher of children and youth. See Figure 1 on previous page.

History of Staff Development

The early history of staff development was simple (Dillon-Peterson, 1991). From the middle of the 1600s until late in the 1700s, professional needs of educators were not complex. The schoolmaster (usually male) had near autonomy with respect to curricula and teaching methods. "Inservice training" was the term in general use. Occasional inservice activities were designed to correct deficiencies in subject matter, but if schoolroom responsibilities were performed with impeccable morals and fiscal competency, the public was satisfied. As schools became more standardized and complex during the 1800s, teacher institutes were provided to make educators more knowledgeable about curricula and more sympathetic toward the individual student's needs (Schiffer, 1980).

The 20th century ushered in an era of increased demand for skilled teachers. Teacher institutes were replaced with extension courses, summer school sessions, after-hours classes, and correspondence studies for educators. Teachers had more control over the type and quality of inservice given, and staff development became a vehicle for growth for the entire school staff. Teacher centers became new providers of the resources that teachers came to regard as important for carrying out their responsibilities more effectively. With the arrival of the 20th century and the evolution of schools as vehicles for a huge agenda of social and cultural needs in a global world, educators became more aware of their need for professional development to help them prepare the nation's citizens for the future.

The term "staff development" was not in general use until the mid-1970s, (Dillon-Peterson, 1991). Dillon-Peterson credits a few far-sighted superintendents with recognizing the importance and the potential of staff development for making significant changes in educational programs.

During the past 2½ decades, staff development has undergone a paradigm shift (Sparks, 1994). Three powerful ideas shaped this movement: 1) results-driven education; 2) systems thinking; and 3) constructivism. According to Sparks, these ideas were fueled by several shifts:

1. From individual development, to both individual development and organizational development;
2. From fragmented improvement efforts, to clear, coherent, strategic plans for the entire school system;
3. From training in sites away from work, to multiple forms of work-embedded learning;
4. From transmission of knowledge by experts, to teacher study of teaching and learning processes;
5. From presentations by trainers, to professional development by consultation and facilitation services;
6. From accountability for staff development by a few, to responsibility for staff development by all; and
7. From staff development as an expensive frill, to staff development as essential and indispensable for preparing students to be productive.

With such ideas as catalysts, hopefully the days of viewing staff development as purposeless, irrelevant, unorganized, impractical, dull, and patronizing are over. Staff development opportunities exist today in virtually every educational community, and there is usually at least one individual assigned to oversee this increasingly important professional activity (Dillon-Peterson, 1991).

Research on Staff Development

Publications focusing specifically on research in gifted education staff development are minimal. Two special issues of *Gifted Child Quarterly*, (1977; 1986) and one issue of *Roeper Review* (1983) featured teacher training and staff development. *Journal for the Education of the Gifted* has published articles on guidelines for professional preparation, college coursework, and teaching standards for educators of gifted students. Maker (1975) and Kaplan (1979) made early contributions to inservice, staff development, and training needs. A few gifted education books authored in the 1970s, 1980s, and early 1990s (for example, Newland, 1976; Maker, 1986; Sisk, 1987; Clark, 1991; VanTassel-Baska, 1992), included a section on personnel preparation.

Joyce and Showers (1983), among others, have proposed frameworks for structuring staff development. Recommended research topics include: 1) effective staff developer behaviors; and 2) coaching in staff development. Later research by Joyce and Showers (1988) indicates that virtually all teachers can learn powerful and complex teaching strategies if the staff development is designed properly.

Wood and Thompson (1993) have strong words for educators in stressing that staff development programs must be built on a set of assumptions grounded in research and best practice. They contend that the minute educators stop their own education, they start down the road to incompetence. The school itself, not the district must be the primary focus of staff development, and the school culture must be supportive of improved practice and growth. Significant change in educational practice will take considerable time over several years. Perhaps most powerful of all is their assertion that staff development should enable school personnel to improve their professional practices in ways that increase student learning. Thus staff development must focus on those things research indicates are related to improved student outcomes. It must support instructional and program improvement and be closely linked to instructional supervision, teacher evaluation, and curriculum implementation (Wood & Thompson, 1993).

Some believe staff development research has been hampered because teachers do not feel they can justify selecting a single goal for professional growth. Rather, they wish to maximize gains across multiple goals for many students. West (1977) describes staff development as an interdisciplinary process with broadly defined goals, but researchers tend to avoid complex goals, unwieldy populations, long-range results, and broad outcomes. Also, research on staff development usually occurs at the local level and is not disseminated widely. All of these factors are magnified when staff development research for complex fields such as gifted education is the issue.

Notwithstanding, a knowledge base does exist and is growing steadily for staff development in general education. Overall advancements in staff development during the past 25 years have occurred in great part through the catalytic effect on teaching generated by emergence of that strong research base (Loucks-Horsley, 1994). Also, a growing body of staff development literature discusses adult learner characteristics, theories of adult learning, instructional frameworks, and adult learner assessment and monitoring. For example, researchers find that participants in staff development experiences want to be involved in learning that is meaningful and applicable to their jobs as professional educators. A base of information is emerging on individual and group attitudes toward the current use of particular innovations proposed as content for staff development activities. Hinson, Caldwell, and Landrum (1989) identify a number of best practices in staff development, including participant involvement in planning, activity-oriented components, and concrete, specific examples. Some research focuses on needs assessment such as the Concerns-Based Adoption Model (Hall, George, & Rutherford, 1977; Roberts & Roberts, 1986). Some years ago Hord (1982) stressed the usefulness of the Concerns-Based Model.

Useful information about the general topic of staff development is available through the work of a number of investigators, including Joyce and Showers (1988), Wood (1989), Loucks-Horsley (1989), Sparks and Simmons (1989), and Caldwell (1989). Several organizations and publications specialize in descriptions and analyses of staff development, and gifted education personnel can learn much from these sources. One of the fastest-growing and most influential organizations for educators' professional development needs is the National Staff Development Council (NSDC). In 1970, the fledgling

NSDC hosted a conference on staff development, with an attendance of 17. Twenty-five years later, NSDC membership numbered more than 7,000, with conference attendance typically exceeding 2,000 (Yastrow, 1994). These yearly conferences focus on research and best practices in staff development, such as the 27th annual conference for 1995 with its mission of "Navigating the Winds of Change," featuring sessions on ensuring leadership for new directions, embracing the strength of diversity, using staff development to improve curriculum and instruction, and creating sustained professional learning communities.

NSDC produces the *Journal of Staff Development,* a publication of timely, cogent material for directors of staff development, teachers, college professors, school board members, school administrators, and others interested in school improvement. NSDC also has established national standards aimed at giving schools, districts, and states direction in determining quality staff development. *Educational Leadership,* a periodical of the Association for Supervision and Curriculum Development (ASCD), often focuses upon staff development issues. Journals such as *Teacher Education and Special Education, Journal of Teacher Education,* and *Journal of Psychological and Educational Consultation* often contain professional development research and theory.

Through the efforts of NSDC and other professional bodies envisioning staff development as a catalyst for change in schools and education, almost all school districts of any size now routinely budget for staff development and seldom introduce a new educational initiative without a staff development component (Brandt, 1994). In his article "Reflections on 25 Years of Staff Development," Brandt summarizes staff development during the past quarter century by noting that there has been:

A. Change from invisibility or non-existence to institutionalization;

B. Upgrade from orphanhood to demands for ownership and collaboration;

C. Significant movement from emphasis on deficit to emphasis on growth and change;

D. Change from emphasis on individuals to emphasis on the group or organization; and

E. Improvement from random selection of focus to more systematic delivery of instruction incorporating principles of adult learning and use of technology.

In reflecting on the past 25 years of inservice and staff development and making recommendations for the future, Wood (1994) emphasizes that teachers are not the only professionals needing to be involved in programs of continuous improvement. Professional development staff must include those responsible for supervision, evaluation, and curriculum development and implementation.

Guskey (1994), an influential leader in professional development, states that staff development is making a difference, but there is still a long way to go to close the gap between its current knowledge base and general practices. Fullan (1994) challenges that staff development is still too divorced from the life of organizations and not yet connected strongly to everyday work. He suggests that when more powerful models are available, policymakers will cease to regard staff development as a frill.

Staff development for all education contexts is an area of great opportunity that needs continued research and development (Joyce, Bennett, & Rolheiser-Bennett, 1990). Many areas in education are underanalyzed as potential sources of information about the effects of inservice and staff development on student learning and teacher development, and gifted education is one such area.

Staff development goals for gifted education are complex, populations are unwieldy, and outcomes are necessarily broad. Studies must be long-range if they are to be meaningful. Research often tends to be carried out on a short-term basis at a local level, with little or no dissemination of results that might help others.

Joyce and Calhoun (1994) propose that staff development is on the verge of becoming THE KEY to professionalization. They point out that staff development is now a field, with policies and a literature base, rather than simply a collection of a few people with vision. They summarily emphasize that the staff development field must continue to grow beyond slick workshops (dubbed "dog and pony shows" by some) that fail to bring about change. The next step, say Joyce and Calhoun, must be staff development for all during built-in time, not for a few volunteers on a catch-as-catch-can basis. It must activate real change, and its effects on students must be assessed.

Differentiating Inservice from Staff Development

Inservice and staff development are two necessary but distinctly different facets of personnel preparation. Inservice is used to help school personnel get specific information and techniques with regard to particular curricula, educational concepts, or school programs. It tends to be a single event or a series of short sessions presented for teachers by persons from outside the local system. In gifted education it is most often conducted by an expert in gifted education who may be a professional consultant, university professor, or teacher in a school-based program. Sometimes inservice is provided by a district administrator or governmental agency staff member and occasionally includes parents and students. Inservice goals for gifted education generally are directed toward cultivating awareness of gifted learners' characteristics and needs, transmitting information about procedures such as identifying gifted learners, and introducing strategies that can help gifted students maximize their potential. At the conclusion of inservice, participants usually evaluate the presenters and assess the relevance of the presented material to their needs by responding to a checklist of questions.

Staff development, on the other hand, is typically a long-term, multi-year process targeted at school goals. Staff development is based on several assumptions, namely that: 1) teaching is an evolving, dynamic profession; 2) educational agencies are responsible for at least part of the professional development of their personnel; and 3) changes for significant improvement will require planned intervention.

Whereas inservice is one component of staff development, a staff development program requires the establishment of goals, local leadership, extensive involvement of school administrators, careful planning based on needs assessment data, collaborative decision making to build ownership, design of appropriate inservice opportunities and other experiences to address perceived needs, and long-range evaluation of effects, with follow-up based on the evaluations. Goals for staff development focus on involvement, commitment, and renewal. Participants determine their own needs in relation to those goals, develop personal steps for professional growth, and evaluate their individual progress toward the goals.

One term to avoid when describing inservice and staff development is "training." The concept of training is more appropriate for efforts to instill particular habits, such as training animals to perform specific acts. Perhaps teachers might be "trained" to make lesson plans in a specific way (Newland, 1976), but a training process per se is not compatible with philosophy and practices that facilitate professional growth and personal development of educators. Effective staff development is a key component in a district's plan for improving school-based education for students. Asayesh (1993) points out that Guskey and other staff development experts have stressed the continuity of staff development. It is ongoing and often built into the school structure, with consistent follow up and support a key component of its success.

Format for Staff Development

Diverse formats for staff development should be considered. As just a few examples, staff developers might consider reading and discussion groups, peer coaching, video- and audio-taping and analysis, observations of other programs, and professional meetings.

Reading and discussion groups are an economical means of staff development. For example, small groups would be supplied with various articles, pamphlets, chapters, books, or journals on the desired topic. Ample, but not too lengthy, time frames would be set up for digesting the readings. The discussion should take place in a comfortable setting, away from distractions as much as possible, with a discussion moderator and a good supply of materials and refreshments.

Another possibility is having staff observe other programs and come back to share their observations and reactions with colleagues. This activity contributes information about potential problems, useful techniques, and helpful resources. Many professional groups can assist

- Professional meetings and conferences
- Educational agency presentations
- Classroom observation and interviewing
- Field trips to sites of gifted programs, mentorships and internships, and community resources for class curricula and individual study
- University coursework in education of the gifted or specific area
- Presentations by consultants, teachers, administrators, mentors
- Seminar programs by experts in content areas
- Technology training by business and computer experts
- Released time to prepare teaching units and curriculum outlines
- Study of professional journals and books
- Development of information and awareness packets
- Collaborative preparation of new teaching materials
- Interviews with students and parents
- Small group discussions on a regularly scheduled basis about—
  - book chapters,
  - research articles from journals,
  - application articles from periodicals,
  - papers from meetings and classes,
  - news articles on timely topics of educational interest, and
  - television shows on educational issues
- Communication with other schools via electronic bulletin board
- Peer observation and coaching
- Video satellite presentations such as those conducted by the National Research Center on the Gifted and Talented
- Collaborative development of classroom materials
- Brainstorming sessions
- Preparation of case studies for analysis
- Development of handbooks and resource notebooks
- Veteran or novice teacher interactions
- Development of games, role plays, and simulations
- Technical assistance programs
- Staff role exchanges
- Mini-course modules
- Service center programs

**Figure 2: Examples and Formats
for Inservice and Staff Development**

professional growth with printed materials as informational resources. Some may offer presentations at a reasonable cost. Such activities are viable alternatives to formal inservice and staff development. It is important to include a variety of activities in order to retain participant interest and involvement.

The development of meaningful inservice or effective staff development is limited only by unimaginative thinking and rigid school structures. Seminar programs can be offered by experts in fields of interest to students and teachers. Exchange programs cultivate rural-to-urban and urban-to-rural understanding. Other possibilities include study groups and problem-solving sessions; preparation of packets and materials for events such as county fair exhibits and library displays; educational television programs; interactive video programs; satellite discussions with leading educational figures; share-fairs with all participants bringing favorite ideas; Saturday programs for parents and community leaders; grant-writing workshops; planned interactions between curriculum specialists and teachers. Figure 2 provides suggestions for inservice and staff development formats. Some of the formats are suitable for inservice, and others are more appropriate for the long-term, intensive staff development process.

Formal and Informal Staff Development

Staff development can be formal or informal. Gifted education personnel will find many opportunities for providing each type of service. Formal methods include scheduled sessions, conferences, programs, workshops, presentations, courses, retreats, and other planned activities. Press releases, brochures, and newsletters are also somewhat formal. Informal staff development includes displays, conversations, observations in other classrooms, observation in follow-up, and also on-the-spot consultations and conferences with professional colleagues.

Some activities are formal in one context and informal in another. Staff development programs that include both types are most adaptable to participant needs and local school goals. Figure 3 suggests ways of implementing formal or informal staff development.

Formal	Informal
Ask to be on meeting agenda.	Interact with support staff.
Negotiate with administrators for collaboration time.	Ask to team teach or present in your specialty area.
Develop fact sheets.	Make and post bulletin boards.
Conduct needs sensing and needs assessments.	Contribute information through newsletters and fact sheets.
Feature timely topics.	Provide helpful materials.
Interface with district or state department efforts.	Take colleagues to conferences.
Host leadership institutes.	Collaborate with parent groups and community organizations.

Figure 3: Implementing Formal and Informal Staff Development

Adult Learners and Lifelong Learning

Learning is a lifelong process for everyone, and extended learning is especially needed by educators whose primary mission is to help others learn. Staff development can provide adults with opportunities they need to engage in lifelong learning. However, those experiences must be planned and presented in ways that address adult learner characteristics. Theories of adult development help staff developers understand how adults change cognitively and emotionally as they pass through stages in their lives (Oja, 1980).

Dalellew and Martinez (1988) note that Knowles, expert in adult learning concepts, distinguishes between learning as children through pedagogy (based on the Greek root "ped") and learning as adults through andragogy (based again on Greek roots of "aner" for man, and "gogius" for guide). Knowles (1984, 1980) stresses that adult learners require learning environments and learning agenda which incorporate four major principles of effective adult education in contrast to children's education:

* self-direction rather than dependent learning;

- a problem-centered orientation to learning rather than subject matter focus;
- a time perspective of immediate application rather than chronological age specifications for the tasks; and
- a rich experience base that contrasts with depending on instructors' experiences for the learning.

Dalellew and Martinez (1988) contend that staff development planners too often operate with the pedagogical mind set they employ as classroom teachers, and they must readjust to view participants from an andragogical perspective. They point out that many adult learning theorists believe adults generally are motivated by internal forces, thus participating in staff development to learn more, not to be externally rewarded for attending or denigrated for not attending.

An understanding of adult learning characteristics and principles helps staff developers select the most appropriate learning environments and content. Because they tend to be motivated by intrinsic forces, they respond to staff development goals that are useful for immediate application with their students. Direct, concrete experiences in which they apply the learned information are essential. They need to see results of their efforts and receive accurate feedback and reinforcement for progress toward their goals. Effective staff developers acknowledge the accumulated wealth of experiences among any group of adult learners and use this experience base to help adults help themselves.

Adults tend to resist situations which seem to be an attack on their competence. They learn best through concrete experiences where they can apply what is being presented and through informal situations where social interactions take place (Wood & Thompson, 1980). Some fear change and new demands to a great extent. They will be more receptive to content designed to convey respect and trust for them as capable individuals.

Adult learners should be consulted in decision-making about staff development. This kind of partnership is necessary for staff developers to gain insight into prior learning experiences of the participants and define current problem areas (Cranton, 1989). Adult learners need practical, focused help; options and choices; efficient use of their time; arrangements that provide for their comfort, and follow up on applications of the staff development content. With these realities in mind, staff developers must make every effort to provide safe but challenging atmospheres for adult learners (Cranton, 1989; Rogers, 1989).

Staff Development with an Inclusionary Perspective

Educators are becoming increasingly sensitive to the need for inclusionary visions and perspectives within the learning environment. Inclusion is to be perceived as contexts and processes for learning, not specifically the places in which the learning is to occur. The inclusionary philosophy "celebrates diversity, promotes accountability and professional collaboration, recognizes the importance of strong social relationships among children, and explores strategies for pursuing excellence without sacrificing equity"(Schrag & Burnette, 1994, p. 64).

Inclusive schools are those that include students with special needs in the total school experience, rather than exclude them in more restrictive settings (Dettmer, Dyck, & Thurston, 1996). Staff development programs which are inclusive in context, process, and participatory roles can help prepare educators for integrating inclusionary perspectives and approaches into all school programs, including those that focus on the needs of gifted and talented students.

Even as inclusionary perspectives are emerging and inclusive schools are becoming more prevalent, different regions of the country are becoming more dissimilar in significant ways. During the next several decades, the nation's schools, colleges, and universities will be called on more and more to meet the needs of diverse populations. Educators must become more knowledgeable about cultures, customs, and beliefs in order to facilitate learning for every individual. Multicultural education can provide the avenue by which we may acknowledge the purposes of education for all persons, understand the rationale for identification of special needs among diverse populations, implement appropriate instructional processes that address each individual's learning needs, and provide suitable curriculum content for the needs of culturally diverse groups of gifted students (Kitano,

1991). Staff development activities that emphasize multicultural education will provide opportunities for professionals to acquire knowledge of other cultures and to cultivate deeper awareness of their own personal biases in interacting and collaborating with professional colleagues (Evans, 1993).

According to Gollnick and Chinn (1991), not only blatant biases, but subtle biases as well, must be recognized and addressed. Gollnick and Chinn identify several important components in fostering a multicultural learning environment. First, teachers need to develop skills in using textbooks and other instructional materials essential for promoting the value of diversity. Teachers also should take steps to ensure that understanding of exceptionality and appreciation for cultural diversity are fundamental parts of the learning environments they structure for students. They need to know where and how to locate supplemental teaching materials, information, and visual aids that encourage appreciation of diverse cultures and individual differences.

Data from a study by Solomon and Levine-Rasky (1994) that explored educators' perspectives on multicultural education policy and practice within schools indicate that teachers express need for relevant content in three predominant areas: 1) race and ethnospecific information about students; 2) pedagogical strategies for classroom use; and 3) competence in working with diverse groups. They want to understand cultural differences and similarities among groups and to become familiar with appropriate curricular materials. They expect inservice to heighten awareness of how their unintentional behaviors might have unintended negative consequences. They also wish to examine their own biases and attitudes toward multicultural perspectives.

When planning and implementing learning activities that can promote adult learners' valuing of diversity, staff developers should model respect for individual differences of the participants and incorporate strategies into the inservice and staff development activities that are appropriate for adult learners. The steps listed in Figure 4 can help staff developers provide experiences that cultivate respect for differences and nurture appreciation of the benefits of diversity. Staff development experiences then will become models for the inclusive perspective that participants will want to take back to their own school settings.

1. Arrange the agenda to have something for everyone.
2. Allow sufficient time for all participants to receive and give information.
3. Structure the environment to facilitate interaction while accommodating individual preferences with style and format.
4. Present information in multimodal format.
5. Pace interaction so all points are covered and no one's input is overlooked.
6. Model support, encouragement, and appreciation for each person's contributions.
7. Strive to have each person receive the kind of outcome he or she values.
8. Encourage selection and use of materials that recognize and respect diversity and promote the constructive use of individual differences.
9. Provide resources (people, places, and things) that celebrate differences.
10. Model appreciation for attitudes, interests, and orientations of participants.

**Figure 4: Using Adult Differences Constructively
in Staff Development**

Foundation for Gifted Education Staff Development

National Excellence: A Case for Developing America's Talent (OERI, 1993), a comprehensive report on the status of gifted education in the United States, presents seven key directives for gifted education. One of the seven is the need to emphasize teacher development. Professional development is essential in preparing educators to provide the challenging curricula and varied learning opportunities that gifted and talented students must have to develop their potential.

The most import variable in determining the success of educational approaches for gifted learners is the teacher (Callahan & Renzulli, 1977). Nevertheless, preservice personnel preparation programs seldom, if ever, contain any specific coursework in gifted education. It generally is not required for educational licensure and credentialing. Study of gifted learners and the differentiated education they need is seldom included in textbooks or lectures, and appropriate education of gifted learners is addressed, for the most part, in specialized graduate studies that are undertaken by only a few. Furthermore, general educators and other support staff rarely receive such information during their formal training. In studies conducted by the National Research Center on the Gifted and Talented, researchers found that classroom teachers did little to differentiate education for gifted learners (Westberg, Archambault, Dobyns, & Salvin, 1993; Archambault et al., 1993). They found very little differentiation in instruction or curricular modification for 84 percent of regular classroom activities in which gifted learners participated. According to Renzulli and Reis (1994), staff development is vital for preparing teachers to use strategies such as curriculum compacting.

In 1994, only 17 U.S. states reported having mandated training leading to teacher endorsements in gifted education (Council of State Directors of Programs for the Gifted, 1994). Finally, school administrators typically are not active participants in gifted education coursework or staff development activities.

Staff developers need to know what is being taught in teacher preparation and school administrator preparation programs so that their roles in facilitating gifted student learning can be addressed. Westberg et al. (1993) stress that responsibility for providing appropriate learning activities to gifted students in general classroom environments should not rest solely with the classroom teacher. Administrators, gifted education program specialists, reading specialists, math supervisors, guidance counselors, and other school personnel share responsibility in differentiating education for gifted learners. Therefore, staff development for gifted education programs must include all educational personnel. However, at the present time the primary vehicles for professional preparation in gifted education that target school-based teachers and administrators are the occasional, short-term inservice activity and the infrequent focus within a staff development event.

Gifted education personnel currently have limited effects on general classroom curricula for gifted students. Because gifted education facilitators generally have been prepared to work with gifted students and not to collaborate and consult with classroom teachers and administrators, staff development experiences must address skill development in consultation and collaboration.

Purposes of Staff Development

Staff development serves one or more of five overarching purposes. Refer again to Figure 1, page 2. They are:

- *Job retention.* Inservice or staff development credits may be required for certification renewal or endorsement for assigned roles.
- *Role modification.* Staff may be asked to alter the scope of an existing role; for example, a facilitator for elementary-level gifted education programs may be assigned responsibilities for the secondary-level gifted education program, as well.
- *Professional development.* When school reforms such as inclusion and outcomes-based education, or school program modifications such as the Schoolwide Enrichment Model or the Multiple Talents Model are adopted, school personnel need

information and skills to help them deal with the changes.

- *Personal growth.* As lifelong learners, educators seek more knowledge and new skills that will help them facilitate students' learning. For example, teachers may want to learn how to compact curricula, or to use trade books with gifted students as a supplement to basal readers. They also value opportunities to focus on time management, relief of stress, and other topics related to their personal welfare.
- *Inspiration.* Educators can be stimulated and energized by motivational inservice and staff development experiences.

Each of these intended outcomes is important for staff developers to address and should be identified at the outset of planning. Modes of delivery will differ according to the purpose of the staff development.

The ideal staff development plan for gifted education programs at all age levels will include at least one, and usually several, of the following:

- Promoting awareness of gifted student characteristics and learning needs;
- Increasing positive attitudes toward gifted students and their unique qualities;
- Expanding teachers' knowledge of content appropriate for gifted student's learning;
- Generating enthusiasm for curriculum differentiation;
- Building a repertoire of teaching strategies that maximize potential for gifted behavior;
- Enhancing skills for teaching and advising the very able and talented;
- Integrating gifted education within the total school curriculum;
- Nurturing a collaborative spirit and skills among professional educators, families, and community members;
- Providing information about resources for facilitating learning; and
- Contributing to the overall mission of renewal and revitalization of education throughout the total school program.

Guskey (1985) asserts that effective staff development will produce three positive outcomes. The first outcome to be achieved is change in the teachers' classroom practices. These modifications then bring about changes in student learning outcomes. Only then do teacher beliefs and attitudes change, as a result of the student outcomes that emanated from the altered teaching practices.

In the late 1970s and early 1980s, advocates for gifted education staff development identified three groups of educators typically present at most inservice activities: 1) the faithful, who have a moderate level of awareness, are positive toward the philosophy underlying gifted education, and are ready for advanced training in diversified strategies; 2) the neutral, who demonstrate little or no awareness and need expanded knowledge and teaching ideas to increase their success with gifted students; and 3) the reluctants, who have negative feelings toward gifted students and any differentiated learning arrangements for them.

Reis and Westberg (1994) highlight the potential of the Guskey approach for effecting teacher change in attitudes. For all three groups of educators who typically participate in inservice activities—faithful, neutral, and reluctant—Guskey's model for teacher change is a promising approach to planning staff development for education of gifted and talented learners.

Shepard (1995) stresses that teachers who are unfamiliar with new curriculum expectations cannot be expected to adopt one-time advice-giving about unfamiliar educational concepts. Instead, they must have relevant experiences with the concepts in their own classrooms before they are comfortable incorporating them into their curriculum frameworks. Teacher practices do change as they see students change and become more productive. This affects their beliefs and attitudes positively, and they become more committed to implementing the curriculum modifications.

Participant Role Groups in Staff Development

Staff development in gifted education provides members of various role groups with basic awareness, knowledge, and skills for nurturing the unique abilities of gifted and talented students. Each person who understands the importance of differentiated education and environments can increase the effectiveness of educational programming for gifted learners. For example, librarians need to be mindful that most gifted learners are capable of reading literature well above their age level and across broad ranges of interest. Parents should understand the dissonance in cognitive and psychosocial development experienced by many gifted students. Administrators must acknowledge the importance of flexible course scheduling to accelerate gifted students' learning programs productively. Community members can advocate support for gifted education programming and services to gifted learners through such options as mentor programs. Gifted students can give needed input into addressing the kinds of learning activities that will help them most.

Each role is a key to the comprehensive education of gifted students. Therefore, each role should be included as a participant in gifted education staff development. Broad categories of role groups to be reached through inservice and staff development activities or informational sessions are:

- *Teachers.* Preservice teachers, novice (beginning) teachers, and experienced classroom teachers; preservice teachers, novice (beginning) teachers, and experienced teachers of gifted students; special education teachers; teacher educators in higher education programs for teacher preparation.
- *Administrators and supervisors.* Superintendents; principals; supervisors and coordinators; special education directors; state department of education/provincial representatives; cooperating teachers for supervised teaching experience.
- *Policymakers.* Legislators; school board members/trustees; board of governors/provincial officials.
- *Higher education personnel.* Not only faculty who teach courses, but those at teaching, administrative, and supervisory levels who design teacher preparation programs, consult with school districts and work with community organizations and parent groups to improve education.
- *Parents.* Parents of gifted students; parents of other students.

- *Students.* Students identified as gifted; other students.
- *Ancillary and support personnel.* Educators in special services such as counselors; psychologists; librarians; media specialists; health service staff; paraprofessionals; social workers; security personnel; custodial, secretarial, food service, transportation staff.
- *Service and community groups.* Mentors; artists; technicians; business leaders and industrialists; medical and dental professionals; youth workers; talent coaches; leaders of avocational and service organizations; retired and senior volunteers; college students; legal professionals; disabled veteran groups; university personnel.

Participation in gifted education staff development is a two-way process. Professional educators for schools, including preservice (in preparation), novice (beginner), and veteran (experienced) teachers, have considerable knowledge and many experiences to contribute to the adult learner setting, as well as much that they can gain from such experience. They can expect to benefit from interacting with others and sharing their ideas. Those in support roles in and out of schools, including community members, parents, and school support personnel, also have knowledge and experiences to contribute and much to gain. Their experiences combine to form a panorama of perspectives through which to engage student learners and serve their diversified learning needs. In turn, they expect to learn more about schools, education, and students as they contribute their talents and share their experiences.

Preservice teachers and novice teachers complete the student teaching requirement and enter the teaching profession with little experience and much anxiety about classroom management. "Will I be able to control the class?" "How can I provide for each student's individual needs?" "How can I possibly get everything done?" "Will my colleagues respect me?" "Will my students respect me?" Not knowing who is typical and what is normal, they are less secure in recognizing special needs and less confident in designing curricular modifications for students with exceptional ability. These new educators have much enthusiasm, energy, and knowledge of the latest trends and methods.

However, they need time to develop an understanding of individual differences, and they should have follow-through and feedback to hone their budding skills. University and college instructors are key personnel for preparing beginning teachers to work effectively with gifted students.

Experienced teachers are more capable of identifying student variability and differentiating learning experiences. They may have had several highly able students in their classrooms and noted their progress, or lack of progress, throughout subsequent school years. However, these veteran teachers may have developed patterns of teaching and classroom organization that teach to the middle, ensuring order and organization in their classes, but failing to maximize the potential of atypical students. They may be less comfortable with, and more skeptical of, new philosophies such as flexible pacing, curriculum compacting, and facilitating learning experiences beyond the school ground. Cramond and Martin (1987) found that values and attitudes expressed by teachers toward academic brilliance do not change very quickly and, unfortunately, seem to reflect attitudes expressed decades ago by adolescents toward academic brilliance. They propose that experienced teachers may be uncomfortable with gifted students or may simply be mirroring the values and attitudes of society at large, which have not changed much toward the highly able. These teachers need updated information and plans for tried-and-true strategies that will showcase their success with gifted students. Collaborative experiences in which they share ideas and receive encouragement from others for their own efforts are effective.

Staff Development Goals

As a result of effective staff development and informational experiences for gifted education programs, participants should be able to:

1. Show respect for the individuality of students;
2. Demonstrate awareness, understanding, and appreciation of society's needs for intellectual and creative production;
3. Commit to enhancing the education of students who have

potential for becoming exemplary creators and producers;

4. Understand variances among gifted students' intellectual, emotional, social, and psychomotor stages of development ;

5. Express a comprehensive philosophy of education that identifies the purpose and goals of the gifted education program and defines exceptional abilities as the program addresses them, targeting student needs to be served, and selecting criteria to assess program effectiveness in serving those needs;

6. Interpret societal attitudes that affect the ways gifted students perceive and are perceived by others;

7. Articulate defensible identification procedures that serve program goals;

8. Determine procedures and instruments for identifying students to be served in programs according to program goals;

9. Implement a defensible policy on identifying and serving gifted and talented students appropriately;

10. Highlight the need for specially trained, qualified personnel to teach gifted and talented students on a regular basis;

11. Clarify roles and responsibilities of gifted education program personnel;

12. Develop skills for planning and implementing curricular modifications that challenge gifted students appropriately in their regular classes;

13. Implement the principles of qualitatively differentiated curricula;

14. Use strategies for integrating the gifted education program into the overall school program through a total team effort;

15. Cultivate collaboration among gifted education program personnel and other school staff through sharing identification responsibilities, relating curriculum content to general education classrooms, sharing materials and techniques, freeing time for differentiated instruction, and reporting student progress to appropriate groups;

16. Foster strong administrative support and involvement in qualitatively differentiated educational programs;

17. Encourage advocacy for gifted and talented students among various client groups;

18. Seek adequate funding, space, and facilities to support the gifted education program as an integral part of the total school curriculum;
19. Develop collaborative partnerships with classroom teachers, counselors, media specialists, medical personnel, mentors, and others; and
20. Promote effective communication and professional development among all in regard to gifted education programs.

Models for Staff Development

Too few models have been developed specifically for gifted education staff development. Model development, implementation, and evaluation are longitudinal activities that often get set aside as busy educators attend to more immediate concerns. However, five models for education in general emerged as effective staff development in the 1980s (Sparks & Loucks-Horsley, 1989). They are: Individually Guided Staff Development; Observation/Assessment; Involvement in a Development/Improvement Process; Training; and Inquiry.

The Individually Guided Staff Development can be as simple as teachers reading journal articles on topics of interest, or more complex such as carrying out special projects supported by incentive grants. Observation/Assessment can include peer coaching, peer observation, clinical supervision, and teacher evaluation. The Involvement in Development/Improvement Process activities might focus on learning while working on a curriculum or school improvement project. Training is to many educators synonymous with staff development (Sparks & Loucks-Horsley, 1989). The goal typically is changing behaviors and transferring those behaviors to the classroom. The trainer provides activities that help teachers achieve desired outcomes. Inquiry staff development may be done by just one teacher or by the total school faculty. It can take a variety of forms, including problem-solving groups, quality circles, and school improvement projects to develop teacher thought (Glickman, 1986).

On more recent and very promising notes for the field of gifted education, a five-year study was initiated by Westberg, Burns, Gubbins, and

Reis for the National Research Council on the Gifted and Talented to investigate professional development practices and their impact on services for gifted and talented students. Studies emanating from experts in the field are identifying exemplary models for staff development and calling for more research and application of the models in schools. Reis and Purcell (1993) present a curriculum compacting study that stresses the need for staff development and preservice training in order to prepare teachers for compacting and enriching the curriculum. Schack and Starko (1990) found significant differences in the preparation for gifted education among teachers of gifted, classroom teachers, and preservice teachers. A qualitative study by Tomlinson et al. (1994) across several institutions identified five themes in preservice teaching experience that are detrimental to understanding and facilitating needs of gifted learners. The findings provide a serious message for faculty in teacher preparation institutions.

In addition, research studies and innovative models for staff development in gifted education are being developed. Clasen and Clasen (1989) address the problem of rural staff development in fields such as gifted education through a telecommunications approach, blending newer technologies such as computers and television with older technologies like phone and mail. The comparison of trained and untrained teachers of gifted students by Hansen and Feldhusen (1994) indicates that teachers who have taken at least three, and preferably five, courses in gifted education are much more effective with gifted students than those who have not received training. The model developed by Feldhusen, Haeger, and Pellegrino (1989) shows that school administrators' participation in a gifted education training program can cultivate support of educational programs for gifted and talented in their schools.

Sparks and Loucks-Horsley (1989) call for continued research to determine the potency of models such as the five general models described above. This call is most timely in regard to staff development for gifted programming. The need for information that will indicate best practices for impact on student learning, relative costs of models, and improvement of teacher competency and professionalism is great.

Consultation and Collaboration for Staff Development

Educational programs designed to serve students' special needs will require collaborative preparation, delivery, and evaluation of curricular differentiation. Team teaching and interdisciplinary instructional planning are two examples of collaboration. Classroom teachers who seek guidance in differentiating curricula are using the process of consultation. Gifted education teachers who gather information from classroom teachers about individual students also are using the consultation process. This professional collegiality promotes shared responsibility and decision-making for the benefit of all students.

Given the nature of inclusion in today's schools, there is an expectation that gifted learners, too, will receive differentiated education in the regular classroom. This expectation places new demands on the roles and responsibilities of classroom teachers, special education staff, and support staff. Thus, it is critical that teachers consult and collaborate with one another to integrate education services for exceptional learners effectively. Gifted education teachers can help classroom teachers develop interest centers for gifted learners or select appropriate supplementary reading materials for them. They may provide demonstration lessons in classrooms and team teach with classroom teachers.

Jakicic (1994) offers several collaboration-focused suggestions for taking small steps in altering school culture:

- Reducing isolation to minimize resistance and feelings of being threatened;
- Cultivating peer sharing that would lead to peer coaching;
- Initiating schoolwide planning to overcome contrived collegiality and balkanization;
- Initiating teacher assistance teams;
- Developing peer coaching plans; and
- Assessing growth collaboratively by observation and feedback.

All school personnel should have knowledge and skills that will contribute toward structuring an integrated learning environment.

Staff development programs in gifted education must be designed to provide professional development in consultation and collaboration. Teacher preparation should contain scenarios for communication and collaboration as well as workshops on team teaching, while staff development activities could model consultation and collaboration through strategies such as peer coaching and teacher assistance teams.

School personnel consult and collaborate when they return from conventions and other professional development events to share with

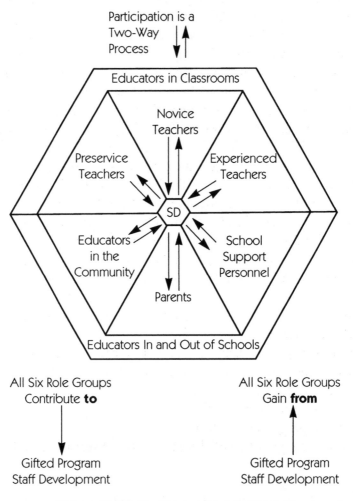

**Figure 5: Role Group Involvement
in Gifted Education Staff Development**

their colleagues what they have learned. They model and peer coach when they demonstrate tried-and-true techniques for colleagues. One group of teachers organized a series of sessions called "THT— Teachers Helping Teachers," in which they alternated in delivering short courses on topics in their fields of expertise. As the sessions became more and more popular, others joined in, and the sessions were carried well beyond each school's boundaries for a positive ripple effect that far surpassed its initial launch at a single school site.

Staff developers are consultants as they initiate their goals (Garmston, 1995). Similarly, consultants are staff developers as they collaborate with consultees to address students' special needs (Dettmer, Thurston, & Dyck, 1993). Consultation and collaboration bring together gifted education and general education and, also, ancillary educational services to facilitate the individualized education of all learners. In a sense, everyone is an educator. Staff development is a two-way process with all educators both contributing to, and gaining from, the staff development (see Figure 5 on page 30).

School-Based Staff Development

When possible, staff development should occur in the school where gifted education programs are to be implemented (Korinek, Schmid, & McAdams, 1985). Having staff development activities at the worksite rather than a neutral location is more likely to improve participation by the faculty. Responsibility and accountability for planning staff development should be school-based and shared by all participating and interested parties, including classroom teachers, principals, and central administration (Wood, Thompson, & Russell, 1981). Mutual understanding by the school faculty is even more important than shared planning and implementation of staff development efforts (Showers, Joyce, & Bennett, 1987). In any case, school-based staff development is recommended over activities at more distant locations.

School-based staff development is a long-term endeavor that takes time—months and even years in some cases. To effect change, the school-based, collaborative staff development approach offers several advantages. Educators and administrators can use collaboration to map out strategies for reaching a goal. The plans may include workshops as well as opportunities to learn and support colleagues who are working to achieve the goal. If the faculty is focusing on a specific goal, personal and material resources can be concentrated in those areas. Assessing progress toward reaching the goals will provide important data to guide decision-making for future staff development efforts.

Consortia for Staff Development

In both rural and urban areas a consortium of schools or school districts or an area resource center, can provide a wide range of staff development opportunities. When resources are pooled through interagency collaboration, staff development can be tailored to role groups or individuals having different levels of experience and needing different emphases.

According to LaBonte, Leighty, Mills, and True (1995), it is not uncommon for one school to be grappling with 15 to 20 change and reform initiatives, many of which operate in isolation. The authors assert that implementing these multiple efforts results only in more meetings, more money required, and unfortunately, little improvement in student learning. They found that whole-faculty study groups initiated within a Focus Team model supporting urban, suburban, and rural schools spread over hundreds of square miles increased collegiality among teachers and influenced the instructional decision-making within the schools.

For specific needs within a particular school or a district, inservice and staff development can be offered at different levels on a single topic. For example, a workshop on curriculum compacting could be set up for teachers who have not used that strategy, while another workshop would be made available for those who have had experience with it but want more information at an advanced level. Another approach would be to have a single workshop, with veteran teachers providing encouragement and guidance for novice practitioners by sharing their experiences and engaging in problem-averting and problem-solving discussions. Other examples of topics that might be needed are, "Ways That Principals and Assistant Principals Can Provide Leadership in Education Programs," "Counseling Gifted Students," and "Differentiating Math Materials for Gifted Students."

As stated earlier, an advantage of the consortium approach to staff development is the collegiality nurtured through communication networks and collaborative interactions. Advocacy groups and regional or state education offices can form alliances with consortia as well. Occasionally, staff development programs can be added to existing education service centers or other educational consortia. In addition, programs can be initiated by groups of gifted education program coordinators who share responsibility for staff development and pool their resources and expertise. A consortium provides a means for using limited resources to enhance staff development. Such opportunities might not otherwise be available to a small school or an isolated district.

Planning Staff Development for Gifted Education

Curriculum differentiation requires that school personnel acknowledge the special abilities and diverse interests of highly able students and develop the competencies to apply the methods and materials that will be needed. The catalyst, or key, for action must be the gifted education facilitator who, along with classroom teachers and sometimes support personnel, sets up learning options, coordinates curriculum alternatives, gathers resources, and designs exploratory activities that will challenge students.

No one staff developer or staff development committee can predict the level of knowledge and extent of skills that educators in a school district already possess or what will make them unsure and uncomfortable in working with gifted learners. However, there are certain aspects of differentiated learning that staff developers can expect to appear consistently. Therefore, it is helpful to consider typical components of gifted education programs so that gaps in knowledge, understanding, and skills can be identified.

Staff development for a gifted program should be perceived as an interactive system of components, including:

- needs assessment;
- definition of the target audience;
- awareness of identification procedures;
- understanding of program goals and learning options;
- staff selection and preparation;
- budgetary matters;
- curriculum development;
- program management; and
- accountability and evaluation.

Each of these components activates specific questions that must be asked about local gifted programming. The critical details of providing differentiated educational services to very able and talented students will include, but not be limited to, flexible pacing, alternative grouping, and challenging curricula. Essentially, gifted programming is shaped by the awareness and the decision making of school personnel in regard to these important issues, each of which necessitates specific actions, and staff development must be constructed to refine such skills.

Increasing school personnel's understanding of the nature of giftedness and related services for learners from preschool through secondary school will help target the necessary elements to include in a needs assessment for staff development. When students have a curriculum presented at a flexible pace (typically, but not always, acceleration), with wider scope (enrichment), using optional structures (primarily student interest-based), then their special learning needs are being addressed. This entails curriculum compacting (having the already-mastered parts eliminated in order to buy time for more challenging activities), or even leaving the school grounds temporarily to engage in mentorships, internships, or apprenticeships. Test-out, dual enrollment, double promotion, peer or cross-age tutoring on an occasional basis, independent study, and small-group projects, are additional possibilities. Many secondary students benefit from rigorous Advanced Placement programs, studying at advanced levels to take tests that can earn them college credits.

Students with varying abilities need to be grouped and regrouped often, in and out of the regular classroom, according to their interests and learning preferences. Many students not identified as gifted also could be in alternative settings for a variety of services on a regular basis—the library for research, the science lab for investigation, the music room for practice and composition, a corner of the cafeteria for a committee meeting, or the playground for practice in social interactions. Sometimes classroom teachers could facilitate these experiences, with the gifted education program facilitators managing the regular classroom. At other times, the gifted education program facilitators should work with gifted students in alternative settings such as a resource room or an off-campus location. Educators must be sensitive to the necessity for personal growth and professional development in order to serve all their students' needs.

Those in charge of the staff development will find that a wealth and variety of materials are available to help with the task and share with teachers to produce positive student outcomes. They include, but are by no means limited to, these sources. Also, a list of additional readings is provided on page 111.

Journals

- *Gifted Child Quarterly* (publication of National Association for Gifted Children)
- *Journal for the Education of the Gifted* (publication of Council for Exceptional Children–The Association for the Gifted)
- *Roeper Review* (published by Roeper City and Country School, Bloomfield Hills, MI)
- *Gifted Child Today* (publication by Prufrock Press)
- *Gifted International* (publication of the World Council for Gifted Children)
- *Journal of Secondary Gifted Education* (publication by Prufrock Press)
- *Parenting for High Potential* (publication of National Association for Gifted Children)
- *Exceptional Children* and *Teaching Exceptional Children* (publications of Council for Exceptional Children)

Books

- *Growing Up Gifted* by Barbara Clark
- *Handbook for Gifted Education* by Nicholas Colangelo and Gary Davis
- *Education of the Gifted and Talented* by Gary Davis and Sylvia Rimm
- *Teaching the Gifted Child* by James Gallagher and Shelagh Gallagher

Best Practices Material

- Curriculum Models by C. June Maker
- Curriculum Development by Joyce VanTassel-Baska
- Enrichment Triad by Joe Renzulli
- Autonomous Learner model by George Betts
- Multiple Talents Model by Calvin Taylor, Carol Schlichter, and Richard Olenchak

Documents
- NRCG/T Research-Based Decision-Making Series
- NAGC Position Papers

Web Sites and Other Electronic Resources
- MonTAGe-TheTAGFAME-Journal (http://www.access. digex.net/~king/tagfam.html)
- CEC ERIC Clearinghouse on Disabilities and Gifted Education (http://www.cec.sped.org/ericed.html)
- Search ERIC Database (http://ericir.syr.edu)
- SEMNET Home Page (http://www.neca.com/~semnet/)
- Jacob K. Javits Gifted and Talented Education Program (http://inet.edgov/progr_info/Javits/index.html)
- The Education Program for Gifted Youth (EPGY) (http://www~epgy.standford.edu.epgy)
- NAGC Home Page (http://www.nagc.org/)
- Talented and Gifted Bibliography (http://klingon.util. utexas.edu/TAG/TAG_Bibliography.html)
- U.S. Department of Education (http://www.ed.gov/)
- Duke University Talent Identification Program—TIP (http://www2.interpath.net/sbi/tip/)
- National Research Center on the Gifted and Talented (http://www.ucc.uconn.edu/~wwwgt/nrcgt.html)
- Gifted Resources Home Page(http://www.eskimo.com/ ~user/kids.html)
- Center for Talented Youth (http://www.jhu.edu/~gifted/cty.html)

Listservs
- TAGFAM listserv (listserv@maelstrom.stjohns.edu)
- GiftedNet—discussion of curriculum for gifted learners (listserv@listserv.cc.wm.edu)
- WMCURRIC-L—discussion of Wm & Mary curriculum for high ability learners(Inboy@facstaff.wm.edu)
- TAG-L—discussion of general issues in gifted education (listserv@vm1.nodak.edu)
- TAGFAM—discussion and support for families(listserv@ sjuvm.stjohns.edu)

- GTOT-L—discussion of very young children who are gifted (listserv@eskimo.com)
- U-ACHIEV—discussion of academic underachievement (majordomo@virginia.edu)
- OHIOGIFT—local mailing list for discussion of issues in gifted education (listserv@lists.acws.ohio-state.edu)

Other Electronic Resources

- Online Support Group (tagfam@maelstrom.stjohns.edu)
- Kids' Chat (tagkids@maelstrom.stjohns.edu)
- Teens' Chat (tagteens@maelstrom.stjohns.edu)
- The Gifted Child on-line chat group (http://www.cole-group.com/nethaven)

Organizations, Centers, and Agencies

- National Research Center on the Gifted and Talented, University of Connecticut, 362 Fairfield Rd., U-7, Storrs, CT 06260-2007
- American Education Research Association-Special Interest Group on Giftedness & Talent, 1230 17th Street NW, Washington, DC 20036-3078; (202) 223-9485
- National Association for Gifted Children, Suite 550, 17707 L. Street NW, Washington, DC 20036
- Council for Exceptional Children-The Association for the Gifted (CEC-TAG), 1920 Association Drive, Reston, VA 22081
- World Council for Gifted Education for Gifted and Talented Children, Inc., c/o Dr. Barbara Clark, California State University in Los Angeles; FAX (818) 716-0329; e-mail: bclark@calstatela.edu
- Supporting the Emotional Needs of the Gifted Inc. (SENG), James Delisle, SENG-College of Education, 405 White Hall, Kent State University, Kent, OH 44242-0001

Human Resources

- University faculty

- State Departments of Education–Consultants and Administrators
- Regional Educational Agencies–Consultants and Administrators
- Local Gifted Education Coordinators
- Parent Advocacy Groups

After staff developers have become familiar with the knowledge base in gifted education, they must know stakeholders' perceptions about gifted education and their visions for this aspect of education in the future. Understanding the knowledge base and ascertaining the shared vision of a local school district's gifted program can give staff developers the foundation they need to construct a needs assessment for building the staff development program. Often, however, those entrusted with development of the gifted program have not generated a program vision or mission statement. Hence, the staff developer first may have to provide training for that.

The program vision is a roadmap for developing the local programs. A mission statement is composed of the vision, beliefs, enabling principles, and commitments of various constituency groups involved in gifted programming (Hunsaker & Landrum, 1995). These essential values, principles, and assurances provide the foundation for educational programming. The fundamental beliefs delineate the values upon which the mission or vision is based, and the enabling principles are statements about how the mission will be realized. The commitments address specific actions directed to target audiences (parents, students, administrators, teachers, community leaders, and so forth). In essence, the vision or mission statement dictates the functions of the program, the nature of the target groups for whom the functions will be served, and the means for achieving these functions. Therefore, the various aspects of the vision or mission statement for the local gifted program will guide educational decision making about the evolution of the emerging program.

Because a mission statement serves as a roadmap for development of the program, it also should guide the evolving staff development program. Therefore, before initiating the staff development plan, the mission should be in place. Then and only then can it have an impact on staff preparation. For example, the mission can help direct staff development leaders in designing needs sensing and needs assessment tasks. The vision or mission for gifted programming becomes the foundation on which staff development is built. The first step in that process is matching the intended outcomes or vision to the design of the needs assessment.

Needs Sensing to Prepare for Needs Assessment

Two processes—needs sensing and needs assessment—are imperative for matching staff development to participant needs. The first, needs sensing, uses a set of techniques to ascertain things about gifted students and gifted education programs that participants may not realize they need to know. Needs sensing data contribute to a more effective, efficient development of appropriate needs assessment procedures. For example:

- What do the participants already know about gifted students and gifted education? What do they want to learn?
- How will they be involved in teaching, counseling, and providing support for gifted students in classroom, co-curricular, and extra-curricular activities? How will they be involved in planning, presenting, and evaluating the staff development activities?

Methods for sensing participant needs include: observational data from classes and other school activities; dialogues initiated to learn about teacher concerns; interviews with students, parents, community leaders, and educational support personnel; and visits to successful programs followed by comparative analyses to determine local needs. Examples of needs-sensing questions are:

1. What do we need to know about our students in order to help them develop their potential to the fullest?
2. How can we determine the kinds of curriculum options and alternatives that will best meet students' needs in ways that work in our setting?

3. How might we use ancillary and support personnel to the best advantage for the learning experiences of our exceptionally able students?
4. Do our current teaching resources extend and enrich the curriculum?
5. How might we determine that the gifted education programs we envision are working (will work) for our school context?

The needs sensing information then should be used to plan formal needs assessment procedures that ensure more individualized, relevant staff development experiences for all participants. For instance, school administrators, who wish to have excellent schools, should value information about gifted education programming which helps them make wise decisions about meeting school district goals. Counselors and psychologists may desire information about the goals and objectives of gifted education programs in order to support those programs. Needs sensing should be undertaken in ways that allow participants of each role group to contribute to this exploratory data collection.

Needs Assessment

The next process is needs assessment, which uses the information gathered from needs sensing to assess participants' priorities and major areas of need. Examples of several needs assessment instruments can be found in the appendices. However, each should be tailored for the particular context in which it is to be used and fine-tuned to the participants' needs and interests.

When planners within one school assess needs, they can be much more specific in determining needs for that context. They will need to determine any discrepancies between school and program goals and where they are currently with respect to local needs. But when staff development involves cooperative efforts among several districts, a task force from the various schools should collaborate in assessing needs and planning the staff development program. Wide variation in maturity and magnitude of programs may exist within and among the districts. Staff development specialists at the district level will need to assess the "state of the gifted education program." Opinions may range from wishing to serve the needs of gifted students in all age ranges and in all content areas to eliminating the program. If a philosophy, set of goals, and defensible curriculum are in place, then needs assessment becomes a guide for soliciting further information. Needs assessment techniques should be designed to gather information beyond opinions, such as examination of program records, placement successes, and achievement in college coursework or on the job. Such information must, of course, be treated as grouped data and not identifiable by students or teachers.

The key elements, therefore, in preparing meaningful staff development that will be more well-received and more likely to be put into practice, should follow the following steps:

- Do a needs sensing of all probable participants.
- Conduct needs assessment based on the findings of the needs sensing.
- Plan staff development that is based on data from the informal needs sensing process and the more formal needs assessment procedure.

Early identification of teacher concerns, obtained through needs sensing and subsequent needs assessment, will facilitate effective planning of staff development content in order to meet participants' needs. The Stages of Concern Model by Hall, George, and Rutherford (1977) illustrates the necessary matches between teacher concerns and inservice and staff development activities. See Figure 6 on page 45. Key questions to ask in planning staff development include, "What do you know about gifted students and gifted education?" "What do you want to learn?" "How will you be involved in teaching, counseling, and supporting or interacting with gifted students in classroom, curricular, and extracurricular activities?" "How are you to be involved in planning, presenting, and evaluating the staff development activities?"

Previous coursework in gifted education, proficiency in targeted content areas, and knowledge of appropriate pedagogy for meeting gifted students' needs should be ascertained with the needs assessment technology. Shared classroom techniques, parent feedback, student achievement, and student attitudes toward school also contribute information. This information can be gathered with needs assessment techniques such as standardized checklists, locally designed checklists or surveys, open-ended surveys of concerns, E-mail discussions, and interviews. Other sources of needs assessment information are teachers' comments, questions, complaints, requests for materials, and reactions to parents and gifted students. Questionnaires or interviews provide information about previous coursework in gifted education, targeted content, and knowledge of appropriate methods for meeting very able students' needs. Parent feedback, student achievement, and student attitudes toward school are sources of data about expertise and need. Parents could be surveyed to provide information about student attitudes toward school and learning. Teachers could observe students in a variety of roles to ascertain their abilities and needs.

Student needs must be considered in all aspects of gifted education program development. Therefore, gifted and students can be called on to provide useful data. Staff development planners will want to observe and talk with students. Students might be asked to complete an interest survey or engage in an interview. In the elementary grades gifted students could be asked to generate their own ideas about components of the gifted education program. The students might draw an "optimal" classroom and label the unique parts or describe their most challenging and inspiring teachers. Students could design their own grading and evaluation systems. They could answer questions about gifted education programs in logs or journals or finish sentences about the program such as, "If I were a teacher of the gifted, I would …" Students might simulate aspects of gifted education programs, and role-play various parts of staff responsibility in those programs. Parents could be surveyed to determine their perceptions of student attitudes toward the program and the entire learning process.

At the secondary level the emphasis moves to student interviews. A safe and open environment must be established, with confidentiality ensured, and the importance of their input should be stressed. They might be interviewed individually, or a student committee could be formed to assess student needs. A student representative could serve on advisory councils or program committees for gifted education.

Stages of Concern*	Typical Expressions of Concern	Suggested Focus for Concerns-Based Inservice
Stage 0 Awareness concerns	What gifted program? I am really not involved with gifted students. I'm too busy with other things.	To arouse interest and provide information about how activities of the program are related to other aspects of the school curriculum.
Stage 1 Informational concerns	I would like to know more about the gifted program.	To provide general information about the gifted program and how it meets the needs of gifted children in short presentations, articles, classroom visits, and conversations with individual teachers.
Stage 2 Personal concerns	How will involvement in the gifted program affect me? What is my role in relation to the gifted program?	To provide information which clarifies role expectations and resolves actual or perceived conflicts between gifted program and other demands on teachers' time and energy. Care should be taken to assure teachers that these concerns are legitimate.
Stage 3 Management concerns	Involvement in the program seems to consume all my time.	To provide information and skills which will help teachers deal more effectively with the day-to-day demands of programs such as scheduling, ordering materials, organizing activities, and to provide opportunities for individuals or small groups to discuss management problems with more experienced teachers.
Stage 4 Consequence concerns	How is the program affecting students? How can I modify the program to increase its impact on students?	To provide information and develop skills related to the evaluation of program impact and to provide opportunities for teachers to participate in professional meetings to refine their skills.
Stage 5 Collaboration concerns	Through working with others I feel that the impact of the program on students could be increased.	To provide opportunities for teachers with collaboration concerns to meet together and exchange ideas and to utilize these teachers as inservice leaders or give assistance to teachers who are less experienced with the program.
Stage 6 Refocusing concerns	I think a different approach would have a greater impact.	To provide opportunities for these teachers to pilot their ideas and use them with less experienced teachers.

*Stages of Concern based on work by Hall, George and Rutherford (1977)
Note: From Roberts, J.L., & Roberts, R.A., (1986). Differentiating Inservice Through Teacher Concerns About Education for the Gifted. *Gifted Child Quarterly, 30*(3), 141.
©1986, National Association for Gifted Children. Reprinted with permission

Figure 6: Matching Teaching Concerns and Inservice Activities

Students might role-play student and staff roles in the program or simulate aspects of the program. Sessions could be set up to talk with staff members. Former students in gifted and talented programs might be interviewed by students, and age peers not in the program surveyed to determine their attitudes toward the program. Parents also should be asked to contribute information. Examples of questionnaires or interest inventories for gaining student and parent input are given in the appendices.

It is important to leave space on a needs assessment instrument for open-ended responses and to encourage them. After needs assessment instruments have been returned, the information should be summarized and used to plan the staff development.

Phases of Staff Development

Staff development is a cyclical process. No single pattern for inservice and staff development will be appropriate for every school context. However, in a typical staff development program four key phases and the major steps within those phases are: 1) preparation; 2) design; 3) implementation; and 4) evaluation. Staff development programs usually are structured in three-year cycles. Within the three-year time frame, the continuous process of preparation, design, implementation, and evaluation is repeated again and again with each staff development effort. Eventually the intended program goals and objectives are met, and then the needs of the school district and its students present new challenges, and the cycle begins again. See Figure 7.

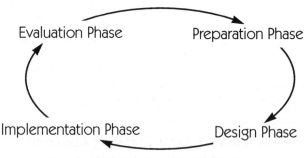

Figure 7: The Staff Development Cycle

Checkpoints for steps in the four phases of the staff development include:

1. *Preparation Phase.* This phase is for data-gathering and decision-making before the actual staff development design is constructed. Staff developers should:
   - ✔ relate staff development opportunities to individual levels of experience and development;
   - ✔ define problems and establish target groups affected by those problems;
   - ✔ establish the need for particular types of training;
   - ✔ determine desired effects of staff development upon program and total school program; and
   - ✔ determine both long-range and short-term goals and objectives.

2. *Design Phase.* This phase involves the construction of a staff development plan to reflect the needs and expectations of the staff. Staff developers should:
   - ✔ keep the goals in mind;
   - ✔ select appropriate materials and resources;
   - ✔ choose activities which address stated goals;
   - ✔ design a variety of activities for integrating multicultural education, accommodating diverse learning styles, setting appropriate instructional pace, expanding levels of learning experiences, and enriching curricular content in relation to the goals;
   - ✔ consider logistics of best times and locations;
   - ✔ ensure that goals of staff development by directing participants toward solutions to problems and objectives for change; and
   - ✔ incorporate a range of staff development opportunities to accommodate staff members' needs.

3. *Implementation Phase.* This phase includes the time spent by participants in working toward staff development goals. Staff developers should:
   - ✔ encourage individual efforts to experiment and take risks;
   - ✔ provide incentives for involvement and rewards for participating;

✔ demonstrate how specific staff development opportunities fit into the long-range plan;

✔ determine the amount of self-directedness appropriate for reaching the staff development goals;

✔ make sure that content and format provide something for all; and

✔ keep the focus of the staff development on student needs and teacher ability to meet those needs.

4. *Evaluation Phase.* This phase involves assessing progress in meeting staff development goals. Staff developers should:

✔ ensure that participants leave with an immediate plan for using training and an opportunity to share results and receive feedback;

✔ meet expectations of each participant insofar as possible; and

✔ motivate participants to work on short-term plans for meeting staff development goals.

Responsibilities of Planners, Presenters, and Participants

Staff development requires time, energy, and commitment from all professional educators. However, three roles are key elements in the process—those of planner, presenter, and participant. Communication, collaboration, and coordination among all three are essential in fulfilling the demanding process of staff development.

Planners of Gifted Education Inservice and Staff Development

The *planner* is responsible for organizing and executing the events. The planner, either an individual or a team, conveys the needs of the participant group to the presenter. If a decision is made to hire an external consultant for the session, certain procedures will help ensure the success of that decision. Suggestions for employing an external consultant are provided in the next section.

Inservice planners should share the results of the needs assessment and anticipated outcomes with the presenters. A phone call to answer presenters' questions should follow. Telephone conversations often yield information about the actual expectations of the school district that may not be conveyed on paper. Some questions to discuss with presenters may be:

- Who are the participants?
- Is participation in the staff development event mandatory?
- Are incentives for participation being offered?
- How is the area/room arranged? Who and how many will attend? For how long?
- Who will produce and provide the handout materials?
- Is the school district following a specific program or curricular model for its gifted education program, and if so, what is it?
- Is this event one inservice in a master staff development plan, and if so, who presented previously, what was said, and what were the reactions?
- What is in place to follow this presentation?

Planners for the inservice, or their designees, have specific responsibilities at every stage of the event as follows:

During the Planning
1. Specify purposes and convey participants' needs to the presenter.
2. Offer to provide handout materials.
3. Request and receive permission before taping any session.
4. Offer credit or other incentives as appropriate.
5. Announce the session and emphasize its purpose to the appropriate audience.
6. Arrange for refreshments.
7. Arrange for environment to accommodate presenter's needs.

Immediately Prior to the Presentation
1. Have requested equipment ready and in good working order.
2. Circulate attendance sheet.
3. Introduce presenter to participants. Cite only two or three

noteworthy facts in order to conserve time for the presenter.

After the Presentation
1. Help presenter pack and remove materials after the event.
2. Arrange for appropriate follow-up communication from presenter to participants.

Presenters of Gifted Education Inservice and Staff Development

Once selected and informed by the planner, the *presenter* designs appropriate activities for the target participants. The presenter's message and delivery must be challenging and substantive. Good presenters have characteristics representative of good teachers and should model teaching practices appropriate in gifted education. The presenter can be one person or a collaborative team from the following areas:

- university staff and teachers from the local district;
- professional consultants in gifted education;
- national leaders in gifted education;
- state or regional educational agency staff;
- researchers and practitioners in the field of gifted education;
- gifted students (a promising idea that should be tried more often);
- leaders of advocacy groups for gifted education;
- members of special interest organizations that support gifted education;
- experts from the arts, medicine, law, education, industry, technology, government, and media; and
- parents of gifted students.

The presenter's expertise in gifted education should be matched with the participants' identified needs and specified goals. Recommendations for consultants whom other school districts with similar program goals have employed are helpful in selecting an appropriate presenter. If possible, the same presenters may be used for follow-up sessions, as too many people presenting different views may be confusing to participants. Another option is to select several presenters having different strengths, specify the goal each is working toward, and explain the relevance of each goal to the long-term staff development plan.

Presenters of gifted education program inservice have several specific responsibilities to participants, which include:

Shaping the Session
1. Obtain clear information about the nature of the inservice session—its purpose, length, participant identity and numbers, and their reasons for attending (especially to ascertain whether voluntary or required).
2. Determine previous staff development on the topic or issue.
3. Know how this staff development opportunity fits into the overall program's staff development plan.
4. Agree on who will produce and provide handout material.
5. Specify equipment needed.
6. Identify a contact person to help with arranging facilities, distributing materials, setting up and testing equipment, and monitoring the time.

Presenting the Session
1. Establish the purpose of the workshop before the event and again within the first five minutes of the presentation.
2. Actively involve participants as much as possible.
3. Evaluate the session from a presenter's point of view to assist future planning. See Appendix I for an example of a presenter's evaluation instrument.

Concluding the Session
1. Provide follow-up and feedback to participants.
2. Improve future presentations based on previous evaluations.

Participants in Gifted Education Inservice and Staff Development
The *participant* is the collective audience. Participants are responsible for being actively involved. They should:

- Strive to gain as much as possible from the experience.
- Use the content soon after the staff development activity.

- Seek assistance in making it work effectively for them and their students.

Specific responsibilities of the participants for the event are:
1. Arrive for the inservice on time and be ready with appropriate materials.
2. Participate with a positive attitude.
3. Plan ways to use information and strategies presented.
4. Provide specific feedback to aid in follow-up activities and evaluation process.

Hiring an External Consultant for Inservice and Staff Development

If an external consultant is hired as an outside expert coming in to help with the staff development program, certain procedures will contribute to the success of this strategy. Staff developers will want to attend to important steps in four key areas when selecting, inviting, making arrangements for, and attending to the needs of an external consultant for inservice or staff development.

1. *Determine needs that the consultant is to address.*
   A. Conduct a needs assessment before selecting the presenter.
   B. Tailor selection of the consultant to assessed needs and priorities.

2. *Generate consultant list.*
   A. Note that well-known names can attract an audience and generate enthusiasm.
   B. Avoid consultants whose primary purpose seems to be selling their own products.
   C. Insist on substantive content that challenges the present knowledge level of participants.

3. *Plan for hosting the presenter.*
   A. Ideally, give the presenter 4–6 months' notice in which to prepare for assessed needs.
   B. Consider collaborating with other districts to minimize costs of the event.
   C. Provide presenters with contracts that include:
      1. Specific services to be rendered
      2. Date, location, and hours of service to be rendered
      3. Confirmation of professional fee and Social Security number
      4. Terms of payment
      5. Expenses to be covered (transportation, meals, lodging)
   D. Confirm plans and arrangements by telephone at least 10 days in advance, including:
      1. Objectives of the presentation
      2. Anticipated outcomes
      3. The day's schedule
      4. Description of audience (grade levels, content areas, awareness level)
      5. Location of lodging
      6. Pickup and transportation arrangements, or road directions if driving
      7. Suggestions for appropriate dress (for weather and for style—casual or more formal)
      8. Mailing address of district contacts
      9. What to do if a cancellation is necessary

4. *Remember common courtesies.*
   A. Remember that the consultant may be alone in an unfamiliar setting.
   B. Be aware that the consultant may need time for rest after traveling.
   C. Do not use school personnel for housing the consultant.
   D. Introduce consultant to person providing transportation to airport upon completion of the event.
   E. Have planner or designee remain with the consultant throughout the day to meet needs as they arise.

Facilitating Gifted Education Staff Development

The content of gifted education program staff development must be selected and presented so that each role group's needs are accommodated. Staff developers should not take a one-size-fits-all approach. Each participant needs specific content and planners should adhere to principles of adult learning regarding participant orientations and prior experiences when structuring the staff development activities.

Content for Gifted Education Staff Development

Some educators are ready for more specialized topics in staff development for gifted programming. Others need to begin at the awareness stage and then progress to deeper levels of understanding and broader ranges of involvement. Content must be is tailored to participants' needs. This means that it might range from insight into characteristics of giftedness and talent, to curricular implications of special abilities, to exposure to curricular alternatives and options, to expansion of competency with subject matter, to selection of appropriate assessment and grading techniques, to locating resources that accelerate and enrich the curriculum, to techniques for conferencing with students and their family members.

Support personnel, including counselors, school psychologists, social workers, media specialists, and others, will value formal presentations in characteristics and needs of gifted students. Paraprofessionals can learn about ways in which to help highly able students learn. Custodians, secretaries, bus drivers, and other school staff can find out about alternative learning programs that take gifted students away from the typical school setting on occasion.

Instructors in arts and technology fields will benefit from information about talents and skill levels of gifted students. University faculty are more likely to provide support in their own fields for gifted education when they know about curriculum design and classroom arrangements that facilitate gifted student learning. Service and community groups can participate in information sessions that increase their knowledge about students and ways they can advocate for gifted education programs. Parents will benefit from information highlighting the need to develop partnerships with their children's school personnel.

Sawyer (1988), Boreland (1989), and others are calling for the field of gifted education to promote more academic rigor in content areas. Sawyer says that this requires teachers to free themselves from the bondage of answer keys and teachers' manuals, living the content of the course rather than merely administering it. These teacher characteristics must begin with colleges and universities in teacher preparation programs and in promotion of teacher excellence and the careful recruitment of future teachers who have high proficiency in their major subject areas.

Bruner (1960) has been critical of education when teachers do not understand their own content areas well enough to recognize high order thinking and creative production by their students. This is not a matter that can be resolved by those in the field of gifted education alone; however, gifted education personnel must be vigilant toward encouraging those who are very knowledgeable and who have a passion for life-long learning to become classroom teachers and school administrators.

Staff development for classroom teachers

Teachers will benefit from awareness activities about different types of giftedness and program options that can be made available for gifted children. They need, therefore, information about identification procedures and their own role in the screening, referral, and evaluation processes of a gifted education program. Teachers also can learn about and practice instructional strategies that differentiate educational opportunities for gifted students.

Topics which surface frequently in needs assessments and have proven to be popular for inservice and staff development planning are listed in Figure 8. They are examples of what might be included as content. The list is representative of typical topics across many different staff development programs. However, it is important to note that the needs sensing and needs assessment procedures, which will be discussed in a later section, must drive the selection of content for the staff development activities. Indeed, these topics could be used as part

Several ideas which can be catalysts for selecting topics on which to construct viable gifted education inservice and staff development programs are:

Skills for Thinking and Producing
Multiple Intelligences
Nurturing Creativity and Talent
Using Effective Problem-Solving Strategies
Developing Critical Thinking Skills
Enhancing Visual Imagery
Cultivating Divergent Thinking Skills
Authentic Learning and Authentic Assessment

Management Skills
Developing Tests that Tap Higher Order Thinking Skills
Facilitating Learning of Gifted Students with Disabilities
Working Smarter, Not Harder, to Meet Students' Needs
Selecting Appropriate Methods for Personalizing the Curriculum
Environments that Encourage Parent Partnerships
Facilitating Students' Independent Study
Modifying Curricula for Individual Abilities and Talent
Compacting Curricula
Improving Skills for Conferencing with Families
Facilitating Peer Tutoring
Expanding Identification and Use of Community Resources

Instructional Strategies
Accommodating Diverse Learning Styles and Interests
Differentiating Assignments and Tests
Designing Alternative Grouping Arrangements
Developing Skills of Inquiry, Investigation, and Research
Questioning and Discussion Techniques
Providing Enrichment Activities
Implementing Cooperative/Collaborative Learning, as Appropriate
Providing Dynamic Teaching To Engage Student Attention and Effort
Building Student Self-Esteem
Augmenting or Replacing Basal Materials with More Challenging Resources
Using Electronic Portfolios for Assessment and Feedback

Other Topics
Developing Appreciation for Cultural Diversity
Using Technology for Effective Teaching and Learning
An Inclusionary Approach to Gifted Education Programs
Securing Grant Funds for Special Projects

Figure 8: Suggested Staff Development Topics

of the needs assessment process by asking prospective participants the areas in which they would like more information and preparation.

Informational sessions for parents

Parents of all students in the schools should have the opportunity to know how the gifted education program addresses characteristics and learning needs of the students it serves. They can obtain information and provide helpful input through participation in needs assessments and discussions at parent-teacher organizations and other community functions, and from reading newsletters and other publications. Parents also need to know how curricula can and should be modified to accommodate their children's abilities and talents in the general classroom, particularly in an inclusive classroom setting.

Parents of students receiving gifted education services should participate in needs assessments, program development, and evaluation and should share information about the program with interested groups. They will benefit from activities that encourage home involvement with the program and show them how to be resources for the gifted education program as well as for the total school program. They should be instructed in effective methods of advocacy and support, for their efforts on behalf of gifted education programs often make a critical difference between program funding and program cuts.

Informational sessions for students

In addition to receiving direct services, gifted students should be involved in needs assessments, peer identification, program evaluation, and advocacy. Awareness sessions can be provided to improve students' capabilities in these roles. Also, as mentioned earlier, interests and learning needs of students must be identified to facilitate the development of a more effective gifted education program. Students can be helped in these sessions to develop awareness and appreciation of their own gifts and talents and the impact of these characteristics upon their lives and society.

Informational activities for the community

Gifted education program staff development opportunities for community members, and others who not only support the programs through taxes but may be called on as resources, as well, can be presented in several forms. Public presentations such as speeches at clubs and organizations will provide the awareness and information that lay a foundation for solid support of programs. News releases and radio and television spots about school programs that address special learning needs of students are helpful if tied to the goal of providing excellent schools for all students. Newsletters, brochures, and informative bulletin boards also can be effective. Community members benefit from information about legislation, program costs, and organizations such as state and national associations. They need resources for learning about gifted behavior, teacher characteristics appropriate for gifted students, and techniques for involving parents.

Needs Sensing: Conduct needs sensing to plan the needs assessment.
Needs Assessment: Engage participants-to-be in needs assessment.
Date and Hours: Determine date and time frame for the sessions.
Topic: Select the topic(s) to be featured.
Content: Select content based on needs assessments and current school issues.
Participants: Determine specific group(s) to be included. (In some instances, this might be undertaken as the first item, preceding needs sensing and needs assessment.)
Title: Choose a catchy, upbeat title.
Presenters: Determine presenter(s) who will conduct the activities.
Incentives: Select incentives, both intrinsic and extrinsic, that stimulate interest and effort.
Publicity: Promote the activities with well-placed, well-designed publicity methods.
Format: Structure format for adult learner characteristics and needs.
Facilities: Plan for adult learner characteristics and content. Sketch a room arrangement, anticipate any problems, and solve in advance.
Materials: Procure or develop materials selectively. Strive for materials of high quality and compatiblity with participants' needs.
Preparation: Assemble materials, double-check details, perhaps rehearse the event.
Evaluation: Prepare evaluation materials. Select methods for obtaining formative information to plan and modify, and summative data for accountability and decision-making purposes.
Follow-up: Determine strategies for follow-up of participants at new needs sensing at a more advanced level.

Figure 9: Staff Development Module Planning Template

Staff Development Modules
for Gifted Education Programs

A planning template for inservice and staff development (Dettmer et al., 1996) will help the staff developer organize and carry out these

Needs Sensing: Staff developer gains information during interaction with curriculum supervisors, administrators, department chairs, parents, and gifted students.

Needs Assessment: Checklist of possible school practices that would serve gifted students' learning needs but, insofar as determined by needs sensing, are not being used currently.

Date and Hours: August 28, 1998, 3:00 p.m.-5:00 p.m.

Topic: Methods for modifying curricula and teaching strategies to facilitate for gifted student learning in inclusive schools and classrooms.

Content: Strategies for curriculum differentiation, including accelerated content, curriculum compacting, flexible pacing, Advanced Placement, enrichment, methods of assessing learning with portfolios and other alternative techniques.

Participants: Curriculum supervisors, department chairs, school principals.

Title: "Turning on the Power of Our Highly Able Students."

Presenters: Nationally known and respected leader(s) in gifted education curriculum. (See page 52 for suggestions on bringing in consultants.)

Incentives: Released time, assurance of full participation by principals, door prize of funds to be used for ordering curriculum materials.

Publicity: School newsletters, article in education section of local paper with photo and write-up about presenters.

Format: A 15-minute overview of gifted learners, half-hour small-group discussion of students' needs, a half hour for audiovisual presentation on methods and materials, a one-hour work session by grade levels and subject areas, small- group presentation of ideas to total group, final small-group session by school to formulate a plan for implementing the methods and obtaining the resources, and a brief total-group review and wrap-up.

Facilities: Pleasant, well-lighted, and well-ventilated area such as a section of the school library, that has work tables, comfortable chairs, and refreshment table.

Materials: Each participant brings texts currently in use, with effective parts for differentiation identified, or notation made that there is none.

Preparation: Arrangements for the consultant. (See page 52. Provide an advance organizer for participants so they will be prepared to bring critiqued texts and suggestions for improvements.)

Evaluation: Questionnaires completed by participants, and by presenters (See appendices for examples.)

Follow-up: Planner conducts phone, E-mail, or personal interviews at 3-month and 6-month intervals after the session, to ascertain progress and determine further needs of participants. If information suggests need for a second session, begin planning.

Figure 10: Example 1—Staff Development Module
for a Curriculum Committee

activities efficiently and productively for all who are involved, see Figure 9. Following the template are four examples of staff develop-

---

Needs Sensing: Information from informal conferences with teachers, classroom observations.

Needs Assessment: Questionnaire asking teachers to check major areas of interest and to add others if needed. (See appendices for examples.)

Topic: Maximizing gifted and talented potential in inclusive learning settings.

Content: Information and examples on characteristics, needs, and curricular implications for gifted students; strategies for differentiating and personalizing instruction; strategies to operationalize the differentiation in an inclusive classroom to benefit all students; methods of assessing student progress; techniques for conferencing with parents of gifted students; and explaining differentiation to non-identified students and their parents.

Date and Hours: October 23, 1998, 8:30 a.m. until 4:00 p.m.

Participants: Elementary teachers (at least one from each grade level).

Title: "Success with Our Students of Exceptional Ability."

Presenters: Gifted education program facilitators.

Publicity: Description of the day's purpose and schedule in faculty bulletin, along with names of those participating; overview of session goals and expected outcomes publicized in information bulletin to the school board.

Incentives: Paid substitutes who have excellent skills and will keep participants' classrooms operating smoothly for the day; lunch; door prizes; credit on salary scale; and invitational letters beginning, "Congratulations! You have been selected by district administrators to have a half-day substitute for your classroom, a fine catered lunch, and the chance for door prizes as you participate in the staff development on maximizing learning for our students of exceptional ability."

Format: All-day session with presenters, lunch, one-hour wrap-up time with presenters, and two-hour sessions in small groups to decide on practices for implementation in own schools and grade levels.

Facilities: Large room with screen for overhead projection. Breakout rooms. Space to display materials brought by teachers and facilitators.

Materials: Participants encouraged to bring one thing—children's book, teaching manual, artifact, picture, or other resource—that they have found helpful in working with high ability students. Gifted education staff also bring exemplary materials and concise instructions about the check-out system for materials that can be borrowed for teachers.

Preparation: Staff developer arrives one hour early to set up the room and make it comfortable, prepare the display space, make coffee and tea, check equipment, and make note pads and writing instruments available.

Evaluation: Questionnaire mailed one month after the session. (See appendices for examples of forms that include questions such as, "What ideas from last month's staff development have you used with your students and what were the outcomes?")

Follow-up: Informal conversations periodically in teachers' workroom, scheduled interactions, and regular classroom visits to encourage teachers to try the content for several weeks and share their ideas with colleagues who did not attend.

Figure 11: Example 2—A Staff Development Module for Classroom Teachers

---

ment and information session possibilities. See Figures 10, 11, 12, and 13.

Needs Sensing: Observations in school setting; discussions with building administrators; conversations with intended participants from a variety of grade levels and content areas.

Needs Assessment: Survey form of questions participants would like to have answered, such as, "What are the schedules of our special education staff, and why?" "What do kids do when they leave our classrooms for gifted education resource rooms or learning centers?" "What should we expect them to do in our classrooms?" "How can I convey to special ed. staff the expectations I have for these students in the regular classroom?"

Date and Hours: September 3, 1998, from 3:30 p.m.-5:30

Topic: Collaboration among general education and special education staff.

Content: The necessarily brief overviews should be accompanied with one-page fact sheets of superior quality and pertinent to each short presentation. The special education director would be the last to present, summarizing the presentation with an integrative handout suggesting ways that inclusive models such as peer tutoring, Class-within-a-Class, cooperative learning, and other classroom structures could help every student be a winner. After a refreshment break, participants ask questions and indicate anticipated needs as they work with exceptional children in inclusive settings. The special education director moderates the discussion, so that all have an opportunity to speak and no one special education presenter handles all the questions.

Participants: All classroom teachers of one building and importantly, all administrators and para-educators (paraprofessionals), if appropriate.

Title: "Teamwork Makes Every Child a Winner."

Presenters: Special education staff for learning disabilities, behavioral disorders, mental retardation, physical disabilities, and giftedness, and special education director if the gifted education program is administered within special education.

Publicity: A basket of treats and overview information about the session, placed in a well-traveled area of the school. (See Figure 18 on page 78 for an example.)

Incentives: Refreshments, selection of an ideal day (not Friday or a day just preceding big school events or holidays), drawings for several coupons with favors such as having the principal as a substitute for a half-day while the recipient visits other schools, having the choice parking spot for a week, or having a $50 petty cash fund available to purchase classroom materials.

Format: A two-hour session with five 10-minute presentations by special education staff that focus on characteristics and needs for learners with emotional and behavioral disorders; learning disabilities; mental disabilities; physical disabilities; and high abilities and talents.

Facilities: Theater-in-the-round or semicircle format. A work station with multimedia potential, or two overheads that allow for presentations with headings on one and subparts on another, can be used. If used, they must be practiced carefully and timed during rehearsal.

Materials: Color-coded handouts to accompany each mini-presentation. In addition, a clear and attractive schedule of the afternoon's session to focus on goals of the staff devel-

---

**Figure 12: Example 3—A Staff Development Module
for a Special Education Collaborative Team**

opment and ground rules for the interaction, such as, "All should have time to speak and receive a response," "No names of students or other identifiers are to be used," "You will have an opportunity to request additional information from and consultation with the special education staff at a mutually agreeable time.

Preparation: Rehearsal is essential. It allows presenters the opportunity to try out material, practice fielding difficult questions, and receive feedback about their handouts. Timing is critical. Running overtime can ruin a good format. The special education director should be a stringent timekeeper, giving a one-minute warning to each presenter and then the stop sign. The rehearsal must be at a time when all presenters can attend, without exception.

Evaluation: An evaluation form to take home and return to special education personnel. There should be an open-ended section for participant responses to questions and comments about specific exceptionalities if they wish to write them.

Follow-up: At the next visit to each teacher's class, special education presenters pick up the evaluation form and initiate further interaction with the participant. Consultation/collaboration conferences can be scheduled at this time, also. Personnel should note which materials the teachers would like to view and topics they would like to discuss.

Figure 12: continued

Needs Sensing: Study of literature on parenting gifted adolescents, conversing with leaders in the field of gifted education who focus on gifted teenagers and on parent involvement.

Needs Assessment: Interviews of a random selection from parents having identified gifted students (including those who opted not to participate in the gifted education program or who participated for a time but then dropped out). Note comments from teachers concerning their interactions with parents of gifted students and parents of students who were evaluated for the program but not placed. Use this information to formulate session goals.

Date and Hours: September 16, 1998, from 7:00 p.m.-9:00 p.m.

Topic: Parent partnerships with schools in addressing concerns surrounding giftedness for students in the secondary gifted education program.

Content: Overview of characteristics, needs, curricular implications, and related problems of very able students in the school context, presented by gifted education staff, then counselor(s), then administrator(s). Audiovisual presentation of students' sharing of their perceptions about giftedness and school. Topics of interest might be: peer pressures; overscheduling; academic and career counseling needs; appropriateness of group learning activities; gifted girls' special needs; perfectionism; underachievement; advantages and possible disadvantages of forming parent groups. Refreshment break, with time for brief perusal of materials, followed by general group discussion to share perspectives, information, and issues.

Participants: Parents of students identified for the secondary gifted education program, and secondary-level building administrators.

Title: "Partners in Maximizing the Potential of Gifted Adolescents."

Figure 13: Example 4—An Information Session
for Parents of Gifted Teens
(Continued on page 64)

Presenters: Gifted education facilitators of the district.

Publicity: Letters mailed from central office to parents (signed by gifted education program facilitator and building administrator), stating the purpose of the session and outlining 2-4 goals of the meeting (such as exploring the option of introducing Advanced Placement courses, encouraging parents to become resource participants in the gifted education program).

Incentives: Refreshments, informational material, book display with opportunity for checking out the materials.

Format: A two-hour session, conducted theater style, with audiovisual station(s) strategically placed for maximum quality presentation, and school personnel sitting among the group, to be spotlighted only momentarily as they are introduced by gifted education staff.

Facilities: Pleasant room to accommodate all participants comfortably. Good lighting for what probably will be an evening session, and excellent acoustics. Non-threatening seating arrangement so all can be seen but none feels exposed. Conveniently placed, attractive display area for books and for handout pickup. A VCR player and TV monitor (two or more if group is expected to be large), with tracking device for fine-tuning to ensure good reception.

Materials: Excellent quality audiovisual, such as "Gifted Children: Dispelling the Myths," produced by the Gifted Association of Missouri, Jefferson City. (This video features high school students who attended the Missouri Scholars' Academy, state department personnel, and exemplary high school- and university-based instructors.)

Preparation: Discussion among gifted education staff, administrators, and counselors, with rehearsal of each group's intended remarks, critique and coaching for smoothing out the remarks and, in particular, anticipation of and practice for handling potentially difficult questions.

Evaluation: Concise questionnaire, with ample space for open-ended comments, to be filled out before leaving the session.

Follow-Up: Letter from gifted education staff, thanking participants and summarizing the session with a positive tone that includes results of the evaluations and their open-ended comments, as well. In this letter the plans for a second session, or some other activity designed to facilitate parent partnerships, can be outlined.

Figure 13: continued

Presentation Techniques

Garmston (1988), a regular contributor to the *Journal of Staff Development* on "The Persuasive Art of Presenting," suggests that a staff development presentation is a present from staff developer to participants. Like a present, he says, the presentation should be selected with its recipients' interests in mind. Usefulness, suspense, and attractive wrappings add to the pleasure of getting a present. (See Figure 14 on the following page).

The Presenter
❑ Accommodates adult learner characteristics
❑ Presents content that addresses participant needs

The Presentee
❑ Participates in good spirit
❑ Commits to trying out the presented content

Figure 14: The "Present"...ation

Time is the most important variable for the staff developer to consider. Lack of time to conduct the activity (from the presenters' perspective), and resentment of time spent taking part in the activity (from the participants' perspective) come up again and again as major sources of frustration surrounding staff development. One group of planners (Tanner, Canady, & Rettig, 1995) formulated a plan that supports a high school's change to block scheduling by providing extended time during the school day for staff development. Principals and teacher leaders build in time within the teaching day without sacrificing instructional time for students. Their calendar planning shows two terms throughout the school year with daily blocks—the 80(10)-80(10) plan, expanded teacher planning in a rotating seven-day cycle, and extended teacher planning blocks in a 4/4 semester plan with one day for teaching planning every four weeks. While such a format cannot work in all schools at all levels, it is virtually certain that creative solutions such as this will be needed to carve out and keep precious time for meaningful staff development.

Attending to small details of convenience and comfort before the staff development activity will set a positive tone. Sending a map in advance—how to reach the site, where to park, and how to find the room—lets participants know they are valued. Arranging for a secure place to put coats, bags, and accumulated materials is another mark of thoughtfulness. Checking on conveniences such as restrooms and drinking fountains shows consideration for participants' needs.

Food is one of the most effective and easily provided courtesies. Health-conscious staff developers offer alternatives to "donuts and coffee," such as fruit and vegetable trays, cheese and crackers, trail mix, yogurt, juice, herbal tea, ice water, and decaffeinated drinks.

Rehearsal
Smith-Westberry and Job (1986) recommend rehearsing an inservice or staff development presentation for timing and cohesion. This is especially important when co-presenters must share a very limited amount of time. Rehearsal also allows presenters to anticipate and deal with emergencies that might come up, such as a burned out bulb on the projector, or an abrasive comment from a reluctant participant, or a jumbled set of note cards. Helpful colleagues can give feedback on presenter inflection, tone, volume, and style of delivery. They can also simulate disruptive events for the presenter to problem-solve, for even the most careful planning and the best intentions can be waylaid by sudden disruptions.

Preparation

Presenters will want to memorize their opening remarks and closing segments, and have an outline of the content in between. If they use note cards, they might write down the opening segment, bullet-point key phrases of the content and then write down the closing segment. Notes or complete text should be typed, triple-spaced to allow for insertions and corrections. A 250-word text requires about 2 minutes to communicate from a podium, or about 1 minute and 45 seconds on radio or television. Speakers should build in "breathers" to allow listeners time to think about a concept and then refocus. When preparing, presenters must remember to keep each point focused on a participant point of view.

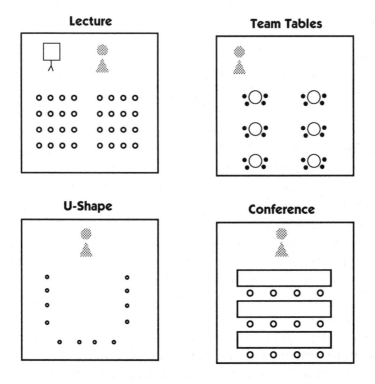

Figure 15: Room Layouts

Room arrangement is important for successful presenting and participating. Size of the group, nature of the content, and equipment used will determine the best physical structure for the staff development environment. See Figure 15 on page 67 for room set-ups that have been recommended by Knowles (1980), Smith (1984), Garmston and Wellman (1992), and others. Comfort level of the presenter is a factor, as well. For example, it is likely that only the most confident and prepared would select a theater-in-the-round structure, and even then it needs a sizable audience for greatest effect. Small semicircles facilitate quick subgrouping into discussion groups. A U-shape format for a small group allows the facilitator to move about from person to person inside the U, encouraging interaction by all. Diagonally arranged tables—sometimes called a "herringbone" design—provide space for participants to work in groups on ideas or products with the presenter moving among them to facilitate their work.

Opening

Presenters should arrive early and ready the room for the event. A transparency can be displayed to greet participants and focus them on the content as they arrive. Sessions should open with an attention-getting device, such as a powerful quote, an arresting display, or a compelling anecdote. This 3- to 5-minute mind set is critical. It should convey the goals for the session, the procedures that will be followed, and concern for participants as valued professionals.

Most importantly, begin on time! If there are to be introductions, they must be kept short. One way to ensure this is to have a brief, personalized "hello" note printed and waiting on chairs to be read as participants get settled, or shown on the overhead as they arrive. If a two-projector set-up can be managed, one screen could provide the "hello" and welcoming comments, and the other could showcase the assessed participant needs and goals for the session.

The bullet-point notes presenters have prepared and rehearsed can free them to connect with the audience and to move about for effect. It is helpful to make eye contact with individuals in the audience who are showing support with their body language and comments; however, all participants should be included by scanning the group often and stepping occasionally into different areas of the room if possible.

Delivery

Many professionals in gifted education have had extensive experience delivering content to a variety of audiences. However, much staff development is taking place at the local level where it is more difficult be "a prophet in one's own land" and establish credibility with peers (Smith-Westberry & Job, 1986). One's teaching colleagues are often the most intimidating of audiences, because they will be around after the event is over and will likely feel free to criticize if the program does not satisfy them in every detail.

Careful organization and rehearsal of material are first steps toward ensuring smooth delivery. Presenters can also take advantage of tried-and-true techniques used by expert speakers and performers to conquer inhibitions and presentation "butterflies." Public speaking experts recommend loosening-up techniques such as lessons in dancing, fencing, or acting; performing dramatic readings or pantomimes in front of mirrors; doing relaxation exercises; overlearning one's material; mastering a few humorous stories *that will offend no one* (not always an easy task to find these); videotaping and self-critiquing for weaknesses such as contradictory cueing or avoidance of certain room areas; enlarging one's repertoire of gestures, examples, metaphors, and group techniques that include boundary-breakers, warm-up activities, choral response or, at times, the dramatic effect of silence. Some presenters watch television or concert performers and copy their performance strategies.

Useful resources for honing presentation skills include *How to Make Presentations that Teach and Transform,* by Robert Garmston and Bruce Wellman, for the Association for Supervision and Curriculum Development; and articles by Garmston in the National Staff Development Council's *Journal of Staff Development,(JSD)* and *The Developer* newsletter. Another helpful resource is William Davis' *The Special Educator: Meeting the Challenge for Professional Growth.* Note Chapter 5, "Preparing and Delivering Talks and Presentations." Garmston's regularly appearing material in *JSD* titled "The Persuasive Art of Presenting" provides valuable information for presenting at one's best. A spring 1993 column featured "Making Nervousness Work for You." "Podium Humor" in the Fall 1993 issue is another. Another *JSD* column, this time by Sharp (1992) and titled "The 'Never-Evers' of Workshop Facilitation" offers cogent tips for having a delightful, not disastrous workshop session. In it the writer cautions presenters to avoid saying they intend to rush through so they can provide more material, or to indicate they would have done something else had there been time.

Visuals

Overhead visuals help presenters order and sequence the presentation. They help avoid omission of key points and save time by keeping the session on track. Participants absorb and remember much more content when it is accompanied by high quality visual materials. However, the visuals must be clear and concise. Color is better than black-and-white, but the most important criterion is size. The presenter should check each visual for size and legibility by standing in the very back of the room, or a comparable room, where it will be shown. This is the time to check on good placement of the screen, as well. See Figure 16 on page 71.

Presenters should not read from the visual, but let participants have time to read it for themselves. When enough time has elapsed, the projector should be turned off to focus attention back on the presenter. To identify a place on the visual, the presenter should point out that place on the transparency, not on the screen itself. Clip on microphones allow presenters to step away from and return to the equipment as needed. Some presenters like to mark on the transparency with non-permanent pens as they speak and participants interact. If so, the impromptu notes must be legible and large.

The best visuals are illustrations and outlines. Tables and charts should contain only information that can be jotted down comfortably while being presented. Other material should be presented in handout form.

Handouts

Handouts, like visuals, must be clear and concise, and color adds appeal. There should not be too many, and they must not detract from the oral presentation. A poor, unprofessional handout is probably worse than none at all.

Closure

Successful presenters stress that one can either ensure or erode the success of the activity in its last moments. Final minutes should be spent summarizing the content and leaving participants with personal commitments to use the material. See Figure 17 for an example of a

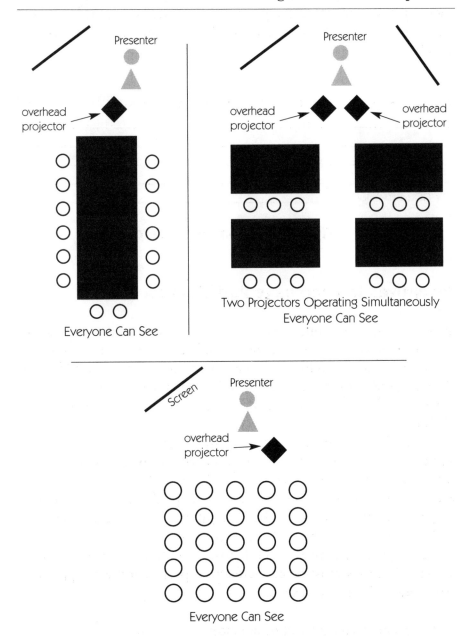

Figure 16: Audio-Visual Layouts

commitment card form. At this time, presenters will want to explain plans for follow-up and give assurances for continued help in implementing the content. Closing comments must be planned carefully and delivered in a positive manner. Most important of all, end on time!

As a result of attending this conference (workshop), I will

_____

_____

_____

_____

by no later than _____

Figure 17: Commitment Card

Incentives to Encourage Participation

Effective staff development is an exhausting, albeit invigorating, activity. Participants must expend considerable time and energy if they are to benefit from it fully. Occasionally, participants need additional encouragement for taking part in staff development activities. A wide variety of incentives can be used, and oftentimes the more inventive, the better!

Released time for teachers to participate in staff development opportunities is a powerful incentive. Participants believe the school administration values the content of the staff development program when it permits educators to engage in professional development activities on work time. Furthermore, participants will not feel that staff development is an add-on responsibility in their already overwhelming job. Incentives for participants can be extrinsic or intrinsic, or both, but they must be cost-effective, specific, and very appealing. Some ideas for incentives are:

- graduate credit (paid or unpaid);
- progress on a local professional growth plan;

- staff development responding to expressed concerns;
- credit on the salary schedule;
- inservice equivalency credit;
- assurance that the inservice will be designed around the needs assessment;
- make-and-take products that will be completed then and there;
- donations of prizes or free services from local businesses;
- choices from which to select sessions;
- name in professional publication;
- a sabbatical for participating in long-term, intensive staff development;
- credit toward annual personnel evaluation;
- a stipend;
- appeal to participants' curiosity, such as a catchy title or an intriguing speaker;
- food;
- door prizes;
- recognition;
- hair stylist or manicurist available, with chances drawn for immediate service;
- priority in using the copy machine or secretarial service for certain days;
- choice space in parking lot during a specified period;
- winning a free class period in which the principal substitutes;
- free materials for classroom;
- assurance that district administrators will attend;
- publicity about the value of each staff development opportunity and its part in meeting school and community goals for educational excellence;
- theater/sports events tickets donated by an interested community member;
- released time to attend;
- substitute provided who will effectively carry out teachers' responsibilities while they are participating in inservice sessions;
- publication of parent requests for staff development that

enhances the school program and enables school personnel to facilitate their children's needs;
- statement from public sources acknowledging the value of staff development for progress in the schools and the community;
- certification renewal;
- coupon for substitute to teach class while recipient observes other classrooms;
- assurance that follow-up support will be provided to participants;
- construction of staff development opportunities from needs assessment data;
- appealing location, such as a retreat or resort area;
- free child care for participants during the inservice;
- coupon for services of art club or vo-tech shop to construct teaching materials;
- presence of a famous person to autograph and speak informally with participants.

Technology to Enhance Staff Development

Technology can enhance staff development in numerous ways. Since a major stumbling block to effective collaboration and teamwork is time, computers and telecommunications can be used to save time in many ways. The "electric bonding" created by technologies such as electronic mail (E-mail), broadcast facsimile (FAX), teleconferencing, and video conferencing will allow participants to communicate with one another quickly and consistently. Information can be collected rapidly and exchanged through databases and electronic bulletin boards. Information on schools can be stored in a file-server and accessed at convenient times. School professionals might enter notes or other forms of information to keep colleagues apprised of items to address or to follow up. Fennimore, Donnelly, and Jones (1988) present a case study of teleconferencing in rural and urban settings to help adult learners assimilate and use complex information. They point out the value of the medium for offering an interactive element and having capacity for live demonstration. They recommend building in time for group activity, reflection on focus questions, discussions with panelists, and break periods.

Karnes and Lewis (1996) provide information on 89 videotapes that cover a wide variety of gifted education topics and are suitable for staff development. They list and describe videos on characteristics, creativity, critical issues, curriculum, identification including preschool and disadvantaged, international perspectives, methods, minority issues, motivation, multiple intelligences, parenting, programming, Structure of the Intellect, talent development, and underachievement.

School personnel can use word processors to collaborate in developing plans, with teacher colleagues accessing the work of others and making changes or adding material. This significantly reduces the time that would be required by face-to-face meetings and generally produces better outcomes, as well. E-mail discussion groups, on-line digital communication, listserve participation, and Internet database access will add to the capability of staff developers to share information, assess participant needs for staff development, and design appropriate content for the activities. E-mail allows information prepared on one computer to be sent by network to another, and some advanced systems are capable of providing real time conferencing. A staff development planning team or follow-up group can save travel time and expense by using such a system. School personnel with modems can engage in communication with large computer information systems. They can search libraries and information bulletin boards to locate methods and materials of meeting teachers' needs. Special bulletin boards can be created to address unique audiences, and it is possible to set up local bulletin boards for teachers in a single school or district.

Digital pagers and cellular phones add to the array of services that staff developers can use in designing and implementing staff development activities. Ideas that have worked in one context can be shared with fellow educators in another (Dettmer et al., 1996).

Technology should not be used to "do the same old thing." It should provide innovative ways of facilitating learning for adults as well as students. For example, software programs for presentations should not be used in place of transparencies, but to extend the content and make it more appealing . Techniques can include quick-time movies, intricate drawings, or HyperCard stacks. Computerized simulations of teaching and learning are promising staff development activities. Use of multimedia technology can greatly increase the sophistication of inservice presentations.

As a part of staff development or as a staff development topic in and of itself, presenters could outline several ways in which participants might work smarter, not harder, with technology as their helpmate (Dettmer et al., 1996):

1. Share survey results of staff use of telecommunications and electronic networks for teaching and collaborating. Then brainstorm ways of augmenting these efforts.
2. Develop time-saving shells or templates for recording and accessing information.
3. Develop databases on topics of general interest and concern in the school district.
4. Create a computerized portfolio as a personal growth activity.
5. Use a computer to adapt instructional plans. At a more complex level, conduct this activity in partnership with several colleagues.
6. Read articles about ways to promote technological literacy.
7. Design a dream-school in which technology would be integral to an inclusionary setting if money were no object.
8. Conduct an inservice on emerging technologies for students' educational programs. Students could be taught skills in computer programming, use of hypertext, and other applications requiring high-order thinking. They might learn how to design programs that solve different types of problems and master basic functions of computer hardware and software. They could use statistical packages to test data from their own projects or those of peers. Many colleges and universities grant college credit for adequate Advanced Placement exam scores on computer knowledge (Pendarvis, 1993).

Productive use of technology by staff developers also can model for educators and prepare the most reluctant to apply technology in their own professional roles. However, staff developers need to plan carefully by asking several questions before selecting a technology tool for an activity:

- Which technology format is available?
- What purpose would it serve in the staff development?
- Can all participants access it when needed?
- Are participants uncomfortable and anxious about such technology?
- How can it be demonstrated efficiently during the staff development?
- Which staff development goals can be addressed by using it?

After using activities that incorporate technology, planners and presenters should assess the contribution of the techniques for future planning. Technology is changing rapidly, and staff developers must remain current with its use. Educators can expect that use of technology in staff development, as well as in classrooms, will increase. Used wisely and competently, technology has exciting potential for facilitating the positive, nurturing environment needed by both adult learners and students.

Promotion and Publicity

Publicity efforts for inservice and staff development programs and for promotion of gifted education programs often overlap. Both kinds of promotion require a positive, professional approach for dealing effectively with reluctant school personnel and community skeptics. Publicity should be planned with care to meet assessed needs and deliver content participants will value.

Misconceptions about gifted children can be overturned by providing extra attention and small courtesies to fellow staff members, parents, and others not directly involved in the gifted education program. When appropriate, gifted education facilitators responsible for gifted education program staff development can share materials and ideas with others. They can extend tokens of appreciation for the interest and efforts made toward gifted education. For example, a small plant can thank a librarian who arranges the use of a corner in the library. A bowl of fruit from grateful parents can be placed in the teachers' lounge, or a surprise bouquet might be delivered to a helpful secretary. Cards of thanks can be sent to the counselor and psychologist, or a note accompanied by a treat might be sent to a support person such as the custodian or bus driver.

Inservice usually is publicized through school newsletters, memos, bulletin boards, parent newsletters, and public address system announcements. Cartoons, quotes, humorous themes, puzzles, or songs can heighten interest. Announcements about inservice might even be placed by a plate of treats in the teachers' lounge, tucked into

Needs Assessment: "Take-a-treat, and leave a sheet"
Leave a basket of candy, cookies, fruit, or other snacks in the teachers' workroom or other place adults gather. School personnel help themselves and fill out a needs assessment form which they leave for the staff development planners to collect.

Information: "Take-a-treat, and take a sheet"
Instead of the needs assessment, have handouts along with treats. These can feature characteristics to watch for, strategies to use, suggested resources, or descriiptions of material

Figure 18: Help Yourself and Your Students

a bouquet displayed in a well-traveled area such as sign-in desk or mailboxes, or lettered on posters made by students and displayed in hallways. See Figure 18 on page 78.

Conferences as Vehicles for Staff Development

Conferences, conventions, seminars, and regional meetings allow educators to bring back ideas for improving education programs in their own districts. However, in the current climate of increasingly tight budgets and accountability for professional time, it has become harder for educators to obtain leave time and financial assistance to attend professional conferences. Nevertheless, conferences are one of the best activities for professional growth, personal development, and inspiration.

Several strategies are helpful in persuading reluctant administrators to provide the time and monetary support to attend major professional meetings.

1. Present or co-present a conference session. This does require taking the time to submit a proposal and is predicated on acceptance of that proposal. Many associations are trying out new ways of showcasing more content through poster sessions, discussion groups, and "marketplace" presentations that enable a greater number of participants to be included in the program and funded by their districts.

    Proposals must be prepared with great care, must feature a topic that adheres closely to the purpose of the conference, and must be submitted on time. The Professional Development Division (PDD) of NAGC has published criteria to guide proposal developers toward success in the proposal review process. Criteria are:
    a. Meets Professional Development Division goals and purposes;
    b. Contributes to division's intent to provide diverse topics and expertise;
    c. Offers significant ideas;

     d. Appeals to the intended audiences;

     e. Represents current thinking in the field;

     f. Is not gimmick-like or prepackaged;

     g. Gives participants practical, useful information;

     h. Makes a genuine contribution to the field.

2. Remind administrators that any session you present can be a publicity vehicle for your district, your students, and your colleagues. Offer to provide publicity material for local media before departing for the convention. A follow-up report that you will provide to the media on your return is a good incentive for receiving approval to go. It is a good idea to carry business cards for networking at convention.

3. Stress the value of the proposal you submitted whether or not it will be accepted. Proposals reflect planning and learning, even when not accepted. Remind your administrators that many good proposals are denied each year simply due to lack of space and limitations of time. State that you will attend sessions in that topical strand to improve and update your proposal, and resubmit it next year.

4. If you will not be presenting at the convention, offer to help the local arrangements committee in some way. Volunteer to chair a session, greet newcomers, facilitate coordination of activities, or staff a booth. It might be a way to reduce costs or to be listed on the program so your district might help with costs.

5 Begin the year before the convention to build networks in your state for collaborating on expenses by sharing transportation and rooms, child care expense, and other burdens of being away from home for several days.

6. Agree to bring back handouts, brochures, materials, lists, or giveaway items for colleagues. Visit the exhibits and examine new products. Take a collapsible box or two and mail the materials from the hotel to cut down on travel burdens.

7. Distribute last year's convention program among colleagues and find out their interests by having them mark topics that would appeal to them if they could attend. At the convention, attend a few sessions that address those interests and

bring back relevant information to share with your colleagues.

8. Keep a journal at the conference. Use it to prepare typed copies of notes you have taken during key sessions and featured speakers. Highlight parts integral to your local area's needs and attach them to your duplicated notes for distribution to colleagues.

9. Present a staff development session for your colleagues on your return, or an information session for your Parent Teacher Organization or school board. Of course, it must be a very productive session so they value the material and feel almost as though they had attended.

10. If none of these is an option, take unpaid leave and tighten the belt elsewhere. The inspiration and enthusiasm you receive may be worth the sacrifice. Then begin to expand your options for the next year and work to realize them.

Professional Development/ Personal Growth Plans (PDPGP)

Many educators are experienced in preparing individual plans for students' special programs. Some participate in Individual Education Plan (IEP) conferences. But rarely do they prepare an individual adult learning plan to guide their own personal growth. A Professional Development/Personal Growth Plan (PDPGP) can be useful for addressing adult needs as a self-directed learner with a wide background of experiences and primary interest in immediate, problem-relevant information. A PDPGP can be a helpful planning tool to set the tone and pace of a staff development experience, and a guide to direct the participant through choices and opportunities. It becomes a self-assessment instrument for determining fulfillment of self-initiated goals and a dissemination vehicle for sharing the learning with others. It models the commitment and effort that teachers expect of students, and it can be satisfying to develop and fun to carry out.

One of the most viable situations for which to create a PDPGP is attending a major convention. Other possibilities are: professional leave to observe and interview in other districts; an exchange program with an educator in another district; or an overseas travel experience. The first step in formulating the PDPGP, just as in the student IEP, is documenting present levels of competence to justify the intended experience as a way of addressing assessed needs. The next steps are to determine specific needs and the time and materials required to meet them. Student needs typically are assessed in academic, social, prevocational, sensory, self-help, and language areas. The adult PDPGP-builder can stipulate personal and professional needs such as greater understanding of giftedness, more awareness of differentiated curriculum alternatives for gifted students, extended skills in implementing strategies, expanded cultural awareness, and increased ability to locate and use resources and materials to develop gifted student potential. These needs become the basis for the PDPGP goals.

Long-term goals apply across the duration of the staff development, with two to four goals appropriate in most cases and one or two measurable objectives by which to demonstrate progress toward goal attainment. Examples of goals and one possible objective are:

1. Acquire information to build home-school collaboration for the benefit of gifted students.
   1.1 Network with individuals from districts with successful parent groups and parent conferencing techniques.
2. Gain a perspective from national leaders about current and future status of gifted education in this country.
   2.1 Attend a featured-speaker session, taking notes for later discussion with colleagues.
3. Refine skills for identifying underserved gifted students.
   3.1 Participate in at least two sessions focusing on underserved populations.
4. Extend ability to provide appropriate curricula for gifted students.
   4.1 After visiting a cross-section of exhibit booths, purchase materials that will interest and challenge gifted students.
5. Enhance multicultural sensitivity through locating new materials and interacting with culturally diverse groups.
   5.1 Compile a list of consultants and possible speakers with

expertise in multicultural perspectives.
6. Cultivate team spirit and camaraderie with participants from own state or region.
   6.1 Have dinner with several colleagues from own area, developing a collaborative network and discussing gifted education in the area.

When outlining the goals and objectives, participants should set aside time and energy, too, for relaxation and rejuvenation, and make allowances for the serendipitous, informal events that often reward educators with the greatest benefits of all.

Then, methods and materials needed to accomplish each goal should be listed. These would include approval for leave of absence, financial assistance if possible, preparations for a substitute, transportation arrangements, passport update if traveling overseas, purchase order for materials to be bought, plans with co-travelers, file and transport system for organizing materials collected, and perhaps preconvention reading on topics to be addressed.

Signatures for the PDPGP may include those of the school administrator who grants the leave, colleagues who will help out during the absence, and family members who will take up home responsibilities during the absence.

Goals and Objectives	Methods	Resources	Time Frame	Evaluation
1.				
2.				
3.				

Figure 19: PDPGP—Professional Development/ Personal Growth Plan

The PDPGP might become a part of the educator's portfolio for annual teacher evaluation. It could be shared with colleagues before and after attending the event, or shown to students as explanation for the absence and model for goal-setting and assessment in life-long learning.

The PDPGP can be recorded on a plan sheet (see Figure 19 on page 83) that includes goals, methods, resources, and evaluation of progress.

The Staff Development Reflective Log concept (Shaklee, 1994) allows adult learners to engage in self-reflection and self-direction as they work on their personal growth and professional development goals (see Figure 20). This technique can be incorporated into most types of staff development activity.

Name_____ Date_____

Highlights of significant learning from the Staff Development Activity (name and describe the event)_____
are:_____

Suggestions for changes/modifications in the next staff development:

Example of what to plan to try next time:

More clarification needed on:

I was surprised that:

I reconfirmed that:

I wonder, question:

Figure 20: Staff Development Reflective Log

Portfolios as Staff Development Tools

Yet another framework for professional development is the portfolio (Dietz, 1995). It is a combination of a working portfolio for assignments, artifacts, and other evidence of prescribed outcomes such as credentialing, and a learning portfolio for descriptions of knowledge, experiences, and feelings. Dietz assembles the portfolio with a structured journal, a folder for artifacts and evidences, a zippered bag, and an optional reflective journal with blank pages. See Figure 21 for examples of elements that might be included in teachers' portfolios.

Goals for self, periodic updates	Self-assessment of progress
Lesson plans that worked well	Videotapes of classroom activities
Supportive notes from parents	Sketches of classroom arrangements
Articles provided for newsletters	Anecdotes about a memorable class-
Sketches of eye-catching bulletin	room experience
boards	Descriptions of good field trips
Samples of exemplary student work	Awards students have received
Rewarding team teaching activities	Original ideas that really worked
Creative assignments and homework	Presentations made at conferences
An effective cooperative learning idea	Helpful comments from others
Notes of commendation from	Ideas shared with others and their
supervisors	comments about using them
Problems met and solved	Best tests and grading techniques
(coded, no names)	Photos of the class engaged in
Products developed using technology	learning

Figure 21: The Teacher Portfolio

Using a PDPGP for a major convention, a reflective log for ongoing experiences, or a portfolio for recording elements of one's teaching can help a staff development participant become focused, and truly learner-centered. These techniques, used as forms of staff development, can be productive and rewarding in many ways.

Evaluation of Gifted Education Staff Development

Evaluation and follow through, two vital components of effective staff development, tend to be neglected more than any other aspect of this important professional function. That is unfortunate, for without continuous assessment it is impossible to know what works and to improve upon what did not. Evaluation should focus both on immediate concerns and on long range goals for improvement and continuation. A first step in conducting meaningful evaluation of a staff development activity is planning it well to ensure that it will be as inclusive and informative as possible. Staff developers will need to address the staff development goals, the format and process, all outcomes, and the cost effectiveness. In addition, it is very helpful to have the needs assessment, the evaluation itself, or both, query participants as to their prior knowledge and attitudes toward the topic so that comparisons can be made.

Castle (1988) provides a six-step evaluation model for assessing effects of the staff development process. She begins with determining criteria and standards, then determines questions based on the objectives. Next is selecting, designing, and administering the instrumentation, followed by analyzing and interpreting the data and stating conclusions. The last two steps are disseminating results and conclusions to all concerned parties, and making decisions based on the results and conclusions. The model involves collaboration of a wide range of school personnel, and is both time and cost effective for making data-driven decisions to improve educational programs.

Holdzkom and Kugligowski (1988) propose five purposes of staff development, including ritual (which approximates the familiar inservice concept), confirmation (in which peers share ideas and professional knowledge), skills enrichment, skills development, and skills remediation. With this approach planners must be responsive to multisourced data and participants must share their needs for specific staff development activities.

Evaluation of inservice and staff development can take any one or several forms. The most frequently used evaluation procedure is a questionnaire to be completed immediately following an inservice session. Although this type of feedback plays an important role by allowing participants to react to the experience and presenters to know of those reactions, the information is limited in scope. Opinions about the expertise of presenters, organization of the session, and relevance of its content do indeed convey participants' immediate reactions. However, information about attitudes and viewpoints on the topic before, during, and particularly after a staff development event will provide even more valuable information about levels of concern, effectiveness of the planning, openness to ideas that were presented, and success of the presenter in stimulating positive attitudes toward the topic. Therefore, three phases—the pre-assessment, immediate post-assessment, and follow-through assessment, should be incorporated to provide a comprehensive view. All who are involved, including planners, presenters, and participants, need to be apprised of staff development outcomes.

The immediate post-assessment should contain both specific and open-ended questions. A Likert scale is preferable to yes/no responses. Many evaluators recommend avoiding the option "no opinion" so that participants will be more likely to respond with the kind of information planners need. At least one open-ended, free response question should be included. Informal interviews seeking viewpoints on particular sessions should be a regular part of the evaluation process, as well. See the appendices section for an inservice evaluation form.

Information can be solicited, also, about physical aspects of the learning experience, such as format, time frame, and facilities. Items should be included which ask whether or not the experience gave an opportunity to gain new and relevant information. Other items should inquire about participants' needs for additional training on the topic. Especially important are indications of interest in making classroom changes suggested by the staff development content. The appendices section provides examples of immediate post-assessment questionnaires which incorporate these items.

An often-neglected source of evaluation information is the presenter. A self-evaluation form for the presenter will provide these data as will a written reaction regarding participant responsiveness. Sample formats for these instruments are in the appendices. Included in this material could be the presenter's suggestions for follow-through activities or future staff development topics. If the session generated products such as questions using higher order thinking, lesson plans with differentiated tasks, or promising activities, the presenter should convey this information to the planner or other person in charge of the activity. Follow-through activities need to have been included in the initial staff development plan.

Informal assessment by staff development designers should be ongoing and include categories such as noting comments, perceiving attitudes, documenting materials ordered, tallying requests for information or materials, and describing follow-through efforts. Feedback from parents and students should be solicited, as well. When follow-through activities are planned and arranged carefully, assessment is easier. After a period of several weeks, or perhaps months in some cases, a formal evaluation of progress toward specific goals of the staff development or inservice should take place.

Ideally, the follow-through assessment is a combination of self-report, multiple classroom observations, and individual or focus group interviews with students, teachers, and parents, audio- or videotapes, and interviews with students, teachers, and parents. Other evaluation methodology might include review of sample lesson plans or other instructional materials, teacher portfolios, rating scales, behavioral checklists, and more. Although all staff development groups should be included in the program evaluation, the focus will be on teacher attitudes and outlooks.

Experts have concluded that changed teacher attitudes are noteworthy, but changes in the school personnel's collective behaviors (both knowledge and skills) will have a more direct impact on student learning and, therefore, are extremely important to stakeholders in the staff development program. Overall, changes in attitudes and behaviors can be expected to have a positive impact on students; however, these changes may be interpreted as program accountability.

Teacher behaviors can be measured by many different methodologies. Self-reports can be collected in the form of responses to surveys or questionnaires, diary and journal entries, and personal portfolios. Classroom observations can inform about changed teacher behaviors as compared with control or norm group behaviors. Pre- and post-measures of observed teacher behavior can be monitored for changes over time. The use of multiple observations by more than one impartial observer will increase validity and reliability. Observations might be made in several short increments, or by shadowing a teacher for a longer period of time. Like observations, rating scales and behavioral checklists can be used to collect information about teacher behavior and compare it to a norm group with standardized measures, or to assess the frequency and duration of behaviors. Individual or focus group interviews can be used to assess self-perceptions of changes in behaviors by staff members. This type of evaluation methodology also will produce some indicators of the nature of changes and the barriers that may have limited the impact of the staff development. Recently, it has been suggested that collecting and analyzing teachers' lesson plans and other instructional materials can identify teacher behaviors related to staff development activities. For example, there might be evidence of teaching creative problem solving techniques or strengthening critical thinking processes in content area lesson plans and instructional materials.

Although the focus of the evaluation for the staff development program should be on teachers, some research suggests testing student achievement as a measure of staff development effectiveness. If a staff development goal is teacher growth with behavior changes, how much evaluation emphasis should be placed on student achievement? It may be appropriate to include such measures; however, care should be taken for the impact on staff development in gifted education is unique. For example, many gifted students already achieve at high levels when they are identified. The premise of gifted education is not necessarily that this level of achievement will increase, rather that it will be sustained with the appropriate instruction. On the other hand, some populations of gifted learners have high levels of potential but demonstrate significantly lower levels of achievement and, therefore, increased student achievement is the goal. As another example, many gifted learners produce extremely high scores on traditional tests of achievement, particularly standardized tests. The low ceilings on such tests make measuring student achievement extremely difficult. Therefore, the measurement of increased achievement is not easily accommodated by the standardized tests of achievement that are available in most schools. Perhaps tests of more complex thinking skills or measures showing mastery of advanced content might demonstrate more fully the change in student achievement that should result from the gifted program. Finally, the debate continues over what gifted programs do indeed offer and whether outcomes can be measured by existing measures of student achievement. More non-traditional measures of student achievement as facilitated by improved teacher attitudes and behaviors will be required to address this issue.

When staff development programs focus on changes in teacher skills, then student work products can reflect the effects of the training. Student products might be compared to those of a control group or analyzed over time with pre- and post-assessments. Portfolios of student work would allow evaluation of changes in student products in stages. Locally constructed or commercial rating scales could be used to evaluate student products. Similarly, rating scales and behavioral checklists might be used to monitor changes or frequency of behaviors that could be linked to specific instructional strategies acquired by teachers in staff development programs.

Creating change in teacher attitudes and behavior is a long-term staff development process. A focused series of inservice sessions and activities, along with well-defined feedback and follow-through activities, will increase the likelihood of participant progress. The information obtained during the follow-through phase of evaluation should be used to help plan future staff development. In order for evaluation to be done effectively, sufficient time, equipment, and facilities must be provided for the follow through and the analysis of results. Therefore, the materials, human resources, and other expenses associated with a staff development program need to be included in the gifted program budget.

The effectiveness of staff development evaluation is dependent upon whether or not the process adequately addresses the questions that all program constituency groups are asking. Evaluation methodologies used must be a good fit to the specific evaluation questions. Gordon's plan for matching evaluation questions and sound methodology is presented here as one model that provides such guidelines. Gordon (1991) recommends that staff development programs be

DO! (before the activity)	**DON'T! (before the activity)**
... Learn what participants want and need to know about gifted students and gifted education programs.	... Neglect to clarify dates and times.
... Find out participants' backgrounds and experiences.	... Ignore needs assessment data.
... Select dates and times that suit as many as possible.	... Expect that participants are thrilled to be there.
... Set goals that address particular issues concerning gifted education programs.	... Assume the material will be well-received.
... Remember principles of adult learning.	... Expect all participants to have the same interests, experiences, and expertise with gifted students.
... Be prepared to make modifications in your presentation.	... Assume much OR little prior knowledge.
... Arrive 20-30 minutes early, at least.	... Make do with poor-quality audiovisuals.
... Publicize through appropriate, effective channels.	... Plan too much material.
... Include administrators and other staff.	... Insist on covering a favorite gifted education model if it does not serve participants' needs.
... Check out materials and equipment early.	
... Carry a "survival box" (with spare bulbs, chalk, tape, markers, 3-prong plug, etc.).	
... Prepare teaching videotapes demonstrating activities for gifted students, and promote them during the session.	

Figure 22: Dos and Don'ts of Staff Development

assessed at four levels:

- Level 1—To measure participants' reaction to the program, often done with a questionnaire at the conclusion;
- Level 2—To determine participants' learning, often done with paper-pencil tests, simulations, and other demonstration methods;
- Level 3—To examine how well participants are using the knowledge and skills on the job, as reported by interviews with supervisors; and

DO! (during the activity)
... Begin on time.
... Be enthusiastic.
... Establish an atmosphere of collaboration and acceptance.
... Make eye contact often.
... Use a variety of presentation styles.
... Set guidelines for accommodating questions and remarks.
... Give everyone encouragement to participate.
... Have a good time—it's contagious!
... Have materials in packets for each participant.
... Use activities that allow practice of content.
... Give praise and recognition as warranted.
... Ask participants to submit a few "stumpers" and promise to address them at the NEXT inservice if it is not possible or realistic to do so then.
... Summarize the main points.

DON'T! (during the activity)
... Lecture non-stop for long periods.
... Play the "expert" role.
... Be too simplistic.
... Be unorganized and too unstructured.
... Use jargon.
... Talk down to participants.
... Tell jokes unless you do them well and the material is acceptable to all (not easy!).
... Put participants in embarrassing, awkward or demeaning positions.
... Allow individuals to divert group attention.
... Share confidential information.
... Be afraid to say "I don't know."
... Be judgmental or accusatory.
... Run overtime!

DO! (after the activity)
... Gather up supplies and personal belongings.
... Provide opportunity for feedback and follow-up.
... Thank participants for attending and for being involved.
... Use evaluations to prepare and present better sessions.
... Learn from mistakes and improve upon them next time.
... Follow-up with participants at a specified later date to inquire about positive effects on gifted students.

DON'T! (after the activity)
... Rush away afterwards.
... Neglect follow-up and follow-through.

Figure 22: continued

- Level 4—To ascertain what differences the staff development made, as determined by measures such as decreased teacher and student absenteeism or teacher attrition and student drop-out rates.

Gordon also reminds staff developers that effects of staff development cannot be considered in isolation. Therefore, they need not bear the burden of a total schoolwide or districtwide improvement effort.

Staff development can influence significantly and positively not only a school's gifted education program but the quality of the total school curriculum as well. Such an important educational process must be treated seriously by all role groups. Some problems to be anticipated in providing staff development for gifted education programs include: 1) negative or indifferent attitudes of school personnel toward staff development experiences; 2) time constraints; 3) limited resources; 4) competition with other programs for attention and resources; 5) fallout from weak or otherwise ineffective activities conducted on previous occasions; and 6) political ramifications of any special support for gifted education programs. See Figure 22 on page 92 for Do's and Don'ts.

The Future of Staff Development for Gifted Education

Just as the gifts and talents of young people have the potential to create a better world for all, so do those gifts and talents have the potential to create a better school environment for all. Gifted program staff development in inclusive schools can enhance educators' abilities to provide classrooms and experiences through which all students can learn and grow.

A staff development program will be successful if the sensed and assessed needs of all role groups are used to construct meaningful goals, implement well-developed plans for meeting those goals, evaluate the activities constructively, and follow through the staff development with practical assistance. Staff developers must not construct their staff development philosophy and programs around faulty assumptions. For example, they must not assume that all teachers are at a loss to devise ways of differentiating curriculum and modify learning environments for diverse needs of students. Many teachers do that very well. Many teachers enjoy working with gifted and talented students and have effective strategies for doing so. Not all administrators react negatively to gifted education programs. School board members do not all have a myopic view of gifted education. Not all gifted education personnel use "dog-and-pony shows" as their professional development formats. And most parents are aware that good gifted education programs can take place only in schools that are good for all students.

Wood and Thompson (1993) caution that several other faulty assumptions must be set aside if staff development as a professional tool continues to improve. For example, staff developers cannot assume that staff development is inexpensive. They cannot assume that classroom teachers are the only ones needing it. They shouldn't regard inspirational speakers as always the best, or the cheapest, or the only, method of delivery. Two or three days per year must not be considered enough. Staff development does not have to be a districtwide event. And so forth. Faulty assumptions bring the predictable results of negative attitudes, with few positive effects on professional practice and no significant effects on student learning.

Gifted education facilitators and staff developers will want to attend to several points for enhancing professional development and personal growth as follows:

1. All professional educators must be involved in ongoing staff development.
2. School administrators must be leaders by supporting staff developers' goals and attending staff development activities.
3. Texts for courses in gifted education and resource books must include material on personnel preparation and staff development.
4. More rigorous and constructive methods for evaluating staff development experiences must be put into practice.
5. Research on inservice and staff development must increase and improve.
6. Gifted education practicum experiences must include practice in consultation, collaboration, and planning and implementation of staff development.
7. University teacher educators must provide experiences for developing skills of collaboration and active participation in staff development programs.
8. Staff developers need to be perceived as the visionaries and change agents in their school contexts.

Sparks (1991), a veteran in the field of staff development for many years, asserts that educators are moving now to another conceptualization of what staff development is. In the 1960s and 1970s it was primarily a coordinating function to get staff developers and participants together, and in the 1980s it was a training period by staff developers. The 1990s ushered in a more comprehensive vision of staff development so schools might respond to changes in the world and the challenge for all students to achieve at high levels. See pertinent articles in issues of *Journal of Staff Development* that follow the course of staff development in education during the past 20 years, and predict the influence staff development is expected to have on schools in the years to come. Therefore, staff developers are called on

Legislators and Policymakers Should:
1. Make a long-term commitment to provide the staff support needed for differentiated curriculum to maximize the potential of all students.
2. Develop policies that encourage lifelong learning by adults and students.
3. Refrain from deregulations that erode commitment and enthusiasm.
4. Make regulations governing gifted and talented education reflect current broadening of conceptions of giftedness.

State Education Agencies Should:
1. Advocate strongly for meeting the needs of all exceptional students, including the gifted and talented.
2. Inform local education agencies about appropriate ways to serve gifted learners.
3. Advise local education agencies on effective ways to provide staff development to facilitate the educational needs of gifted and talented students.

Institutions of Higher Education Should:
1. Refine and offer courses needed by general and special education personnel and school administrators in order to serve gifted students' needs.
2. Conduct research on practices of developing, implementing, and evaluating.
3. Serve as consultants to local education agencies and state education agencies on topics germane to gifted education.

Local Education Agencies Should:
1. Define purposes of services and identify a service continuum.
2. Provide differentiated curriculum, rich learning environments, and personalized learning options for students with high potential.
3. Have staff development that prepares all educators to maximize student potential.
4. Collaborate and network with a wide array of service organizations, policy-makers, and other school systems to share ideas and pool resources.

Parents and Communities Should:
1. Establish partnerships with schools.
2. Support staff development that provides professional development and personal growth opportunities for school personnel.
3. Strive for the social excellence that nurtures school excellence.

Figure 23: Excellent Education Requires Effort from All

on to do fundamentally different things as the new millennium approaches.

The field of gifted education has propelled schools and education into many educational changes in the past four decades. Once again the field can lead with vision and openness to change. Mathieson (1989) calls upon staff developers to be people of vision who believe that educators can accomplish almost anything if they set up the right conditions for harnessing power in a positive direction. She challenges staff developers to exhibit five characteristics:

- extraordinary effort;
- a very clear sense of direction;
- ability to deal with failure;
- creative approaches to problem-solving; and
- refusal to be complacent with success.

Educational programs for gifted students will improve when effective staff development becomes a part of the school goals. In addition, countless positive ripple effects should occur throughout the entire school system as a result of successful programs for gifted and talented students. Rich opportunities abound for staff development in a multitude of curricular areas that reflect successes of the past, mirror today's concerns, and predict exciting possibilities for the future.

Educators are familiar with the proverb, "It takes a whole village to educate a child." There is a part for all, and great need for commitment from all. Stakeholders in teacher preparation and staff development for gifted programs are presented in Figure 23, and their most obvious involvement in staff development for gifted education is highlighted. It will take all educators in schools and homes working together to educate our children and youth effectively.

Afterword

This publication replaces an earlier work by members of the Professional Development Division of NAGC that was titled *Staff Development for Gifted Education: Putting It Together and Making It Work,* a publication released by the National Association for Gifted Children (NAGC) in 1990. The present publication reflects current issues pertaining to school reform, accountability, personnel preparation, and competencies needed by those who facilitate the learning of gifted and talented children and youth.

**The Professional Development Division
of the National Association for Gifted Children**

The Professional Development Division (PDD) of the National Association for Gifted Children (NAGC) encourages educators to become involved in the Division, and to support research and development for preparation of gifted education program facilitators and support personnel. The division offers professional development activities at each annual NAGC convention and professional networking throughout the year. Division offices provide opportunities for leadership roles for NAGC. There are opportunities, also, for writing and editing the Division newsletter, articles for NAGC's *Communique,* and service publications such as this handbook.

The Professional Development Division provided leadership and coordination in developing *Standards for Graduate Programs in Gifted Education.* This document was approved by the National Association for Gifted Children in 1995. The standards contain a conceptual framework of indicators to be used in the preparation of gifted education program personnel.

Where to Obtain More Information about the Professional Development Division

Names and addresses of Professional Development Division officers may be obtained from:

Executive Office
National Association for Gifted Children (NAGC)
1707 L Street, NW
Washington, DC 20036
(202) 785-4268

Interested persons may receive information and application forms for becoming a member of NAGC and for joining the Professional Development Division as well as other divisions of the association..

Division Mission Statement

The primary purposes of the Professional Development Division (PDD) of NAGC are to improve the quality of personnel preparation programs in gifted education, and to further the development of leadership within the field of of education for the gifted. Current areas of interest within the division include: (a) inservice and staff development; (b) leadership and administration, and (c) personnel preparation and program standards for higher education.

Division Goals

1. To synthesize and disseminate the information that expands the knowledge base in personnel preparation for gifted education.
2. To encourage emerging leadership and administration skills in the field of gifted education.
3. To advocate for higher quality undergraduate and advanced degree programs in preparing individuals to work with gifted and talented individuals.

Division Membership

Membership consists of members in good standing with the National Association for Gifted Children with expressed interest in, and commitment to, the goals of the PDD Division. Members in good standing have paid NAGC dues and PDD dues. Administrators, teachers, consultants, professors, and those in many other professional roles are represented within the Division's membership.

Those who join NAGC for the first time, or who renew NAGC membership, and wish to affiliate with the Professional Development Division, should place a check by the division's name on the list of NAGC divisions included on the application form, and should add the appropriate fee to the total NAGC dues.

Contact the NAGC Executive Office at the address or phone number above for membership forms. The Professional Development Division is listed as Division H on this form.

Opportunities within the Professional Development Division

The division is responsible for developing the annual conference program strand for topics related to the division's mission statement. Members review proposals and assist the division chair in designing the division's role during the national convention. Members also may elect to become involved in a number of division projects during the year. One such project is the division newsletter. The newsletter is mailed to division members at least twice each year. Another project is the division's Leadership Institute held during annual convention week. Each leadership institute focuses on current issues related to professional development.

References

Archambault, Jr., F.X., Westberg, K. L., Brown, S.W., Hallmark, B. W., Zhang, W., & Emmons, C.L. (1993). Classroom practices used with gifted third and fourth grade students. *Journal for the Education of the Gifted, 16*(2), 103–119.

Asayesh, G. (1993). Staff development for improving student outcomes. *Journal of Staff Development, 14*(3), 24–27.

Boreland, J.H. (1989). *Planning and implementing programs for the gifted.* New York: Teachers College Press.

Brandt, R. (1994). Reflections on 25 years of staff development: Establishing staff development as a professional function. *Journal of Staff Development, 15*(4), 2.

Bruner, J. (1960). *The process of education.* Cambridge, MA: Harvard University Press.

Caldwell, S. D. (Ed.). (1989). *Staff development: A handbook of effective practices.* Oxford, OH: National Staff Development Council.

Callahan, C. M., & Renzulli, J. S. (1977). The effectiveness of a creativity training program in the language arts. *Gifted Child Quarterly, 4*, 538–545.

Castle, D.K. (1988). Evaluating the effects and the process of staff development. *Journal of Staff Development, 9*(1), 20–26.

Clark, B. (1992). *Growing up gifted.* New York: Macmillan.

Clasen, D. R., & Clasen, R. E. (1989). Using telecommunications to meet the staff development and networking needs of educators of the gifted in small or rural school districts. *Roeper Review, 11*(4), 202–205.

Cooper, C.R. (1995). Integrating gifted education into the total school curriculum. *The School Administrator, 4*(52), 8–9, 12–15.

Council of State Directors of Programs for the Gifted. (1991). *The 1990 state of the states gifted and talented education report.* Austin, TX: Author.

Cramond, B., & Martin, C. E. (1987). Inservice and preservice teachers' attitudes toward the academically brilliant. *Gifted Child Quarterly, 31*(1), 15–19.

Cranton, P. (1989). *Planning instruction for adult learners.* Middleton, OH: Wall & Emerson.

Dalellew, T., & Martinez, Y. (1988). Andragogy and development: A search for the meaning of staff development. *Journal of Staff Development, 9*(3), 28–31.

Dettmer, P., Dyck, N., & Thurston, L. P. (1996). *Consultation, collaboration, and teamwork for students with special needs* (2nd ed.). Needham Heights, MA: Allyn & Bacon.

Dettmer, P., Thurston, L. P., & Dyck, N. (1993). *Consultation, collaboration, and teamwork for students with special needs.* Needham Heights, MA: Allyn & Bacon.

Dietz, M. E. (1995). Using portfolios as a framework for professional development. *Journal of Staff Development, 16*(2), 40–43.

Dillon-Peterson, B. (1991). Reflection on the past, present, and future of staff development. *Journal of Staff Development, 12*(1), 48–51.

Evans, K. (1993). Multicultural counseling. In Silverman, L. K. (Ed.), *Counseling the gifted and talented.* Denver, CO: Love.

Fennimore, T. F., Donnelly, D. L., & Jones, B. F. (1988). A case study of video teleconferencing for staff development in urban an rural areas. *Journal of Staff Development, 9*(4), 22–27.

Feldhusen, J. F., Haeger, W. W., & Pellegrino, A. S. (1989). A model training program in gifted education for school administrators. *Roeper Review, 11*(4), 209–214.

Fullan, M. G. (1990). Staff development, innovation, and institutional development. In B. Joyce (Ed.), *Changing school culture through staff development* (pp. 3–15). Alexandria, VA: Association for Supervision and Curriculum Development.

Garmston, R. (1995). You are a consultant before you are a presenter. *Journal of Staff Development, 16*(1), 50–51.

Garmston, R. (1988, October). Giving gifts. *The Developer, 3,* 6.

Garmston, R. J., & Wellman, B. M. (1992). *How to make presentations that teach and transform.* Alexandria, VA: Association for Supervision and Curriculum Development.

Glickman, E. (1986). Developing teacher thought. *Journal of Staff Development, 7*(1), 6-21.

Gollnick, D. M., & Chinn, P. C. (1991). *Multicultural education for exceptional children.* Reston, VA: ERIC Clearinghouse on Handicapped and Gifted Children.

Gordon, J. (1991). Measuring the goodness of training. *Training, 28*(8), 19-25.

Guskey, T. R. (1994). The most significant advances in the field of staff development over the last twenty-five years. *Journal of Staff Development, 15*(4), 5–6.

Guskey, T. (1985). Staff development and teacher change. *Educational Leadership, 42*(7), 57–60.

Hall, G. E., George, A.A., & Rutherford, W. L. (1977). *Measuring stages of concern about the innovation: A manual for use of the Social Concerns Questionnaire.* Austin, TX: The University of Texas at Austin, Research and Development Center for Teacher Education.

Hansen, J. B., & Feldhusen, J. F. (1994). Comparison of trained and untrained teachers of gifted students. *Gifted Child Quarterly, 38*(3), 115–121.

Hinson, S., Caldwell, M.S., & Landrum, M. S. (1989). Characteristics of effective staff development programs. *Journal of Staff Development, 10*(2), 48–52.

Holdzkom, D., & Kugligowski, B. (1988). Measuring the effects of staff development. *Journal of Staff Development, 9*(1), 10–13.

Hord, S. M. 91982). The concerns of teachers of gifted youth: Using concerns to improve staff support. *Roeper Review, 5*(2), 32–34.

Hunsaker, S., & Landrum, M. (1995). *Developing a mission statement for gifted education.* The Annual Conference of the National Association for Gifted Children, Tampa, FL.

Jakicic, C. (1994). Taking small steps to promote collaboration. *Journal of Staff Development, 15*(2), 16–18.

Joyce, B., & Calhoun, E. (1994). Staff development: Advancements in the last 25 years. *Journal of Staff Development, 15*(4), 3–4.

Joyce, B., Bennett, B., & Rolheiser-Bennett, C. (1990). The self-educating teacher: Empowering teachers through research. In B. Joyce (Ed.), *Changing school culture through staff development* (pp. 26–40). Alexandria, VA: Association for Supervision and Curriculum Development.

Joyce, B. R., & Showers, B. (1988). *Student achievement through staff development.* New York: Longman.

Joyce, B. R., & Showers, B. (1983). *Power in staff development through research on training.* Alexandria, VA: Association for Supervision and Curriculum Development.

Kaplan, S. (1979). *Inservice training manual: Activities for developing curriculum for the gifted/talented.* Ventura, CA: Office of the Ventura County Superintendent of Schools.

Karnes, F. A., & Lewis, J. D. (1996). Staff development through videotapes in gifted education. *Roeper Review, 19*(2), 106–110.

Kitano, M. K. (1991). A multicultural educational perspective on serving the culturally diverse gifted. *Journal for the Education of the Gifted, 15*(1), 4–19.

Knowles, M. (1980). *The modern practice of adult education: From pedagogy to andragogy.* Chicago: Follett Press.

Knowles, M. (1984). *The adult learner: A neglected species* (3rd ed.). Houston, TX: Gulf Publishing.

Korinek, L., Schmid, R., & McAdams, M. (1985). Inservice types and best practices. *Journal of Research and Development in Education, 18*(2), 33–38.

LaBonte, K., Leighty, C., Mills, S. J., & True, M. L. (1995). Whole-faculty study groups: Building the capacity for change through interagency collaboration. *Journal of Staff Development, 15*(3), 45–47.

Loucks-Horsley, S. (1994). Significant advancement in staff development of the past 25 years. *Journal of Staff Development, 15*(4), 7–8.

Loucks-Horsley, S. (1989). Managing change: An integral part of staff development. In S. Caldwell (Ed.), *Staff development: A handbook of effective practices* (pp. 114–124). Oxford, OH: National Staff Development Council.

Maker, C. J. (1993). *Critical issues in gifted education: Programs for the gifted in regular classrooms.* Austin, TX: PRO-ED.

Maker, C. J. (1975). *Training teachers for the gifted and talented: A comparison of models.* (Report No. EC082-478). ERIC Document Reproduction Service No. ED 119-453-95. Reston, VA: Council for Exceptional Children.

Mathieson, D. A. (1989, February). Risk-taking for professional growth. *The Developer*, 1–2.

National Staff Development Council. (1991, April). Characteristics of effective staff development activities. *The Developer,* 5.

Newland, T. E. (1976). *The gifted in socioeducational perspective.* Englewood Cliffs, NJ: Prentice Hall.

Office of Educational Research and Improvement (1994). *National excellence: A case for developing America's talent.* Washington, DC: U.S. Department of Education.

Oja, S. N. (1980). Adult development is implicit in staff development. *Journal of Staff Development, 1*(1), 7–56.

Pendarvis, E. D. (1993). In A.E. Blackhurst & W. H. Berdine (Eds.). *An introduction to special education.* New York: Harper Collins.

Reis, S. M., & Westberg, K. L. (1994). The impact of staff development on teachers' ability to modify curriculum for gifted and talented students. *Gifted Child Quarterly, 38*(3), 127–135.

Reis, S. M., & Purcell, J. H. (1993). An analysis of content elimination and strategies used by elementary classroom teachers in the curriculum compacting process. *Journal for the Education of the Gifted, 16*(2), 147–170.

Renzulli, J. S., & Reis, S. M. (1994). Research related to the school-wide enrichment triad model. *Gifted Child Quarterly, 38*(1), 7–20.

Roberts, J. L., & Roberts, R. A. (1986). Differentiating inservice through teacher concerns about education for the gifted. *Gifted Child Quarterly, 30*(3), 107–109.

Rogers, J. (1989). *Adult learning* (3rd ed.). Philadelphia, PA: Open University Press.

Sawyer, R. (1988). Point-counterpoint: In defense of academic rigor. *Journal for the Education of the Gifted, 11*(2), 5–19.

Schack, G. D., & Starko, A. J. (1990). Identification of gifted students: An analysis of criteria preferred by preservice teachers, classroom teachers, and teachers of the gifted. *Journal for the Education of the Gifted, 13*(4), 346–363.

Schiffer, J. (1980). *School renewal through staff development.* New York: Teachers College Press.

Shaklee, B. (1994). *Staff development reflective log.* Paper presented at the NAGC annual convention in Atlanta.

Sharp, P. A. (1992). The never-evers' of workshop facilitation. *Journal of Staff Development, 13*(2), 38–40.

Shepard, L. A. (1995). Using assessment to improve learning. *Educational Leadership, 52*(5), 38–43.

Showers, B., Joyce, B., & Bennett, B. (1987). Synthesis of research on staff development: A framework for future study and a state-of-the art analysis. *Educational Leadership, 45*(3), 77–78.

Sisk, D. (1987). *Creative teaching of the gifted.* New York: McGraw-Hill.

Smith, T. C. (1984). *Making successful presentations: A self-teaching guide.* New York: Wiley.

Smith-Westberry, J., & Job, R. L. (1986). How to be a prophet in your own land: Providing gifted program inservice for the local district. *Gifted Child Quarterly, 30*(3), 135–137.

Solomon, R. P., & Levine-Rasksy, C. (1994). *Accommodation and resistance: Educators' response to multicultural and antiracist education.* A report to the Federal Department of Canadian Heritage. North York: York University.

Sparks, D. (1994). A paradigm shift in staff development. *Journal of Staff Development, 15*(4), 26–29.

Sparks, D. (1991). The future of staff development. *ASCD Update, 33*(4), 2.

Sparks, D., & Loucks-Horsley, S. (1989). Five models of staff development for teachers. *Journal of Staff Development, 10*(4), 40–57.

Sparks, G. M. (1983, November). Synthesis of research on staff development for effective teaching. *Educational Leadership*, 65–72

Sparks, G. M., & Simmons, J. M. (1989). Inquiry-oriented staff development: Using research as a source of tools, not rules. In S. Caldwell (Ed.), *Staff development: A handbook of effective practices* (pp. 126–139). Alexandria, VA: National Staff Development Council.

Tanner, B., Canady, R. L., & Rettig, M. D. (1995). Scheduling time to maximize staff development opportunities. *Journal of Staff Development, 16*(4), 14–19.

Tomlinson, C. A., Tomchin, E. M., Callahan, C. M., Adams, C. M., Pizzat-Tinnin, P., Cunningham, C. M., Moore, B., Lutz, L., Roberson, C., Eiss, N., Landrum, M., Hunsaker, S., & Imbeau, M. (1994). Practices of preservice teachers related to gifted and other academically diverse learners. *Gifted Child Quarterly, 38*(3), 106–114.

VanTassel-Baska, J. (1992). *Planning effective curriculum for gifted learners.* Denver, CO: Love.

West, S. (1977). How research helps staff development: In schools and in big business. In C. W. Beegle & R. A. Edelfelt (Eds.), *Staff development: Staff liberation.* Washington, D.C.: Association for Supervision and Curriculum Development.

Westberg, K. L., Archambault, Jr., F. X., Dobyns, S. M., & Salvin, T. J. (1993). An observational study of classroom practices used with third and fourth grade students. *Journal for the Education of the Gifted, 16*(2), 120–146.

Wood, F. (1994). Twenty-five years of progress and promise. *Journal of Staff Development, 15*(4), 4–5.

Wood, F. H. (1989). Organizing and managing school-based staff development. In S. Caldwell (Ed.), *Staff development: A handbook of effective practices* (pp. 26–43). Alexandria, VA: National Staff Development Council.

Wood, F. H., & Thompson, S. R. (1993). Assumptions about staff development based on research and best practice. *Journal of Staff Development, 14*(4), 52–57.

Wood, F. H., Thompson, S. R., & Russell, F. (1981). Designing effective staff development programs. In B. Dillom-Peterson (Ed.), *Staff development/organizational development. ASCD Yearbook.* Alexandria, VA: Association for Supervision and Curriculum Development.

Yastrow, S. (1994). A history of the national staff development council—25 years of growth and service. *Journal of Staff Development, 15*(4), 12–17.

Recommended Readings

Bailey, G. D., & Bailey, G. L. (1994). *101 activities for creating effective technology staff development programs: A source book of games, stories, role playing, and learning exercises for administrators.* Jefferson City, MO: Scholastic.

Bailey, G. D., & Lumley, D. (1994). *Technology staff development programs: A leadership source book for school administrators.* Jefferson City, MO: Scholastic.

Beach, D. M., & Reinhartz, J. (1989). *Supervision: Focus on instruction.* New York: Harper & Row.

Brookfield, S. D. (1989). *Understanding and facilitating adult learning* (2nd ed.). San Francisco: Jossey-Bass.

Davis, W. E. (1985). *The special educator: Meeting the challenge for professional growth.* Austin, TX: PRO-ED.

Dettmer, P. (1995). Building advocacy and public support for gifted education. In J. L. Genshaft, M. Bireley, & C. L. Hollinger (Eds.), *Serving gifted and talented students: A resource for school personnel* (pp. 389–405). Austin, TX: PRO-ED.

Feldhusen, J. F. (1986). Policies and procedures for the development of defensible programs for the gifted. In J. Maker (Ed.), *Critical issues in gifted education: Defensible programs for the gifted* (pp. 235–255). Rockville, MD: Aspen.

Fenstermacher, G., & Berliner, D. (1983, November). *A conceptual framework for the analysis of staff development.* Santa Monica, CA: Rand.

Gifted Child Quarterly. (1986). [Special focus on inservice and staff development], *30*(3).

Gifted Child Quarterly. (1977). [Special issue on training], *21*(2).

Griffin, G. (Ed.). (1983). *Staff development.* Chicago: University of Chicago Press.

Guskey, T. (1986). Staff development and the process of teacher change. *Educational Researcher, 15,* 5–12.

Hall, M. S. (1988). *Getting funded: A complete guide to proposal writing* (3rd ed.). Portland, OR: Continuing Education Publications, Portland State University.

Journal for the Education of the Gifted. [Issues *12*(1); *14*(1); *14*(4)].

Journal of Staff Development.

Journal of Teacher Education. [Special issue on Preparing Teachers for Cultural Diversity.], *46*(4).

Joyce, B. R. (Ed.). (1990). *Changing school culture through staff development.* Alexandria, VA: Association for Supervision and Staff Development.

Lieberman, A., & Miller, L. (Eds.). (1991). Staff development for education in the '90s: New demands, new realities, new perspectives. New York: Teachers College Press.

Oliva, P. F. (1993). *Supervision for today's schools* (4th ed.). New York: Longman.

Roeper Review. (1983). [Special issue on training programs], *6*(1).

Schlichter, C. L. (1986). Talents unlimited: An inservice education model for teaching thinking skills. *Gifted Child Quarterly, 30*(3), 119–123.

Solomon, R. P. (1995). Beyond prescriptive pedagogy: Teacher inservice education for cultural diversity. *Journal of Teacher Education, 46*(4), 251–258.

Sparks, D., & Loucks-Horsley, S. (1989). *Five models of staff development for teachers.* Oxford, OH: National Staff Development Council.

Szabos, J. R. (1993). Demonstration teaching: Another view. In C. J. Maker (Ed.), *Critical issues in gifted education: Programs for the gifted in regular classrooms.* Austin, TX: PRO-ED.

Toppins, A. D. (1990, November). Going to a conference? How to bring home more than memories. *The Developer, 1,* 4.

Villa, R. A. (1989). Model public school inservice programs: Do they exist? *Teacher Education and Special Education, 12*(4), 173–176.

Appendix A

How can we help with your gifted education needs?

Name _____

School_____

Check Role(s):

    _____ Gifted Education Program Coordinator

    _____ General Education Classroom Teacher

    _____ Gifted Education Self-Contained Classroom Teacher

    _____ Gifted Education Program Resource Teacher

The topics below are often suggested by teachers as problematic, or are new areas in which you may not have had training. Please help us determine how we can best use our district's inservice time by rating the topics as they would be most helpful to you. Place one of the following numbers before each item to reflect the value you place on that item. Use any number as many times as you wish.

5. very important   4. of some interest
3. of minimal interest 2. of no importance
1. not sure—need more information

___Understanding Characteristics of Gifted Students
___Identifying Gifted Students' Abilities and Interests
___Identifying Very Young Gifted Students
___Counseling Gifted Students
___Differentiating the Curriculum for Gifted Students' Needs
___Differentiating Assignments to Serve Individual Needs
___Selecting Appropriate Content
___Communicating With Families of Students in the Gifted
    Education Program
___Communicating With Parents of Students Not Selected for the
    Gifted Education Program
___Serving Gifted Students from Special Populations
___Advocating to the School Board for a Gifted Education Program
___Other?_____

Appendix B

What Are Your Staff Development Needs for Your Gifted Education Program?

Your district's gifted education program personnel have obtained funds for staff development. for personnel in selected schools. Your school(s) and grade level(s) have been selected to participate. A 2-session module will be offered on identifying and serving students whose characteristics indicate high potential for academic performance, exemplary talent, and/or creative production. To address your needs and interests, please respond to the following items and return the form to _____ in _____ by _____.

Check all of the following you would like to know more about. Then rank your selections (1 = highest priority).

Check   Rank   Item

_____ _____   1. Recognizing and encouraging high abilities and creative behaviors of students.

_____ _____   2. Observing signs of high ability among the culturally diverse who are under-represented and underserved in most gifted education programs.

_____ _____   3. Assembling information in portfolios to identify student needs and strengths.

_____ _____   4. Going beyond basal materials to allow students to demonstrate high potential and productivity.

_____ _____   5. Collaborating with gifted education program personnel, support personnel, and teaching colleagues to meet the needs of high ability students.

_____ _____   6. Locating and selecting appropriate materials that extend and enrich learning experiences for exceptionally able students.

_____ _____   7. Compacting curriculum effectively in order to buy time for curriculum differentiation and alternatives.

_____ _____   8. Conferencing with parents of gifted students on matters such as accelerated content, cooperative learning, and grading.

_____ _____ 9. Evaluating the work of highly able, talented, and creative students, and providing constructive feedback for them and their families.

_____ _____ 10.Other(explain)_____.

THANK YOU!

Appendix C

Student Survey of the Secondary Learning Environment

Directions to Students: Rate each of the following statements as to how you perceive your learning environment. Consider all of your teachers and classrooms as a total group when responding.

1—Strongly Agree   2—Agree   3—Disagree   4—Strongly Disagree

_____ 1. Teachers use lecture more than any other teaching style.

_____ 2. Students are allowed to raise questions of real importance to them when discussing subject matter.

_____ 3. Homework and classroom assignments come from textbooks and require little individual problem solving or creative thinking.

_____ 4. Teachers often talk with students about their opinions and real-life situations.

_____ 5. You could learn most or all of the work in your classroom as an independent study (on your own).

_____ 6. When you correctly complete assignments in class, you are usually given more of the same kind of work to do.

_____ 7. You are allowed to bring outside interests into your classroom work.

_____ 8. You are given the opportunity to study more advanced topics in a subject area after you have completed your regular assignment.

_____ 9. Your classroom or homework assignments differ from others in class.

_____ 10. You are given some choice of curriculum content and alternative ways to study material.

_____ 11. Your teachers have expertise in the content area(s) they teach.

_____ 12. You have opportunities to work at your own pace without restriction.

_____ 13. Many of your assignments repeat the same information or skills.

___ 14. Teachers provide different ways to assess/grade your class work.

___ 15. You receive extensive feedback and constructive comments on your work.

Appendix D

Student Interview Questions

Meet informally with students in small groups or individually. Ask questions to elicit information. Allow students to offer comments. Teachers' names are not to be used.

1. What motivates you to do well in a class?
2. What kind(s) of class and homework assignments are most challenging?
3. What is difficult for you in the learning process?
4. How does teaching style affect your learning?
5. What personal qualities make a teacher most effective for you?
6. What kinds of product-oriented tasks are most interesting and challenging for you?
7. To what degree do your classes challenge you at present?
8. What services do you receive now from the gifted education program?
9. What services offered by the gifted education program help you most?
10. What services offered by the gifted education program help you most?
11. What suggestions do you have for providing students with interesting, challenging classes?
12. In what areas do you possess particular talents?
13. Do problems arise due to your exceptional ability and your participation in the gifted education program? If so, how do you handle them?
14. What are your special learning needs that result from your abilities, talents, and interests?
15. What kind of gifted education program would you design?
16. If you could change one thing about the gifted education program, what would that be?

Appendix E

Gifted Education Inservice Evaluation

Your Name (optional):_____

Your Teaching Area(s):_____

Your Teaching Level(s):_____

Inservice Site and Date(s):_____

Inservice Topic:_____

Rating Scale: 3-Considerably   2-Somewhat   1-Very little

_____ 1. The inservice reflected the needs assessment in which I participated.

_____ 2. The inservice increased my understanding of the nature and needs of students with high potential.

_____ 3. The inservice directed my attention to opportunities for maximizing potential of high ability students.

_____ 4. The session(s) provided me with ideas to use in my own teaching situation.

_____ 5. The inservice was presented efficiently and effectively.

_____ 6. The facilities were satisfactory.

_____ 7. Because of the inservice I am more interested in collaboration with gifted education personnel.

_____ 8. I have at least one thing in mind that I will try because of this inservice.

_____ 9. Strengths of this inservice were_____

_____.

_____ 10. This inservice could be improved by _____

_____.

I would like to receive more information from gifted education personnel on_____.

(Be sure to give your name and school address.)_____

THANK YOU!

Appendix F

Evaluation and Follow-through for Gifted Education Staff Development

By taking the time to complete this questionnaire, you will help gifted education program personnel and central office administration evaluate progress toward meeting our school and district goals. With your help we will be able to plan effective staff development experiences to meet teacher and student needs.

1. Have you implemented strategies presented during the staff development? If so, describe briefly, and circle your rate of success and satisfaction.

_____

Will continue it	It was O.K.	Won't try it
3	2	1

2. If you have not used any of the strategies presented, please explain reasons.

_____

_____

3. To what extent have you discussed and compared any of the strategies with teacher colleagues and administrators? Please estimate the frequency and explain any benefits of these interactions.

Frequently		Occasionally		Not at all
1	2	3	4	5

_____

_____

4. Check areas about which you would like more information and assistance.

_____ Nature and needs of gifted students

_____ Gifted potential in culturally diverse populations

_____ Portfolio assessment to demonstrate outcomes and encourage

_____ student-directed learning

_____ Replacing basal materials to meet gifted students' needs

_____ Collaborating with others to address needs of high ability students

_____ Locating appropriate materials to extend and enrich gifted student learning

_____ Compacting curriculum to allow time for enrichment and acceleration

_____ Conferencing with family members of high ability students

_____ Evaluating work of highly able students and giving them constructive feedback

Appendix G

Presenter's Self-Evaluation

Name_____ Place_____
Inservice Title _____ Date _____

Rate the session using the following scale:
5—Excellent, Outstanding   4—Good, Better Than Average
3—Satisfactory, Average   2—Fair, Below Average
   1—Poor, Markedly Inadequate

- To what degree was I prepared?
  1   2   3   4   5
- Did I establish rapport within the first 5 minutes?
  1   2   3   4   5
- Did my material seem to offer new ideas, methods or skills for participants?
  1   2   3   4   5
- Did the material seem to apply to participants' educational setting?
  1   2   3   4   5
- Did they seem to want to know more about this topic?
  1   2   3   4   5
- Did I offer opportunities for participant involvement?
  1   2   3   4   5
- Was I organized?
  1   2   3   4   5
- Were the facilities adequate?
  1   2   3   4   5
- Were the program designers cooperative?
  1   2   3   4   5
- Was I given an accurate description of the audience?
  1   2   3   4   5
- My overall rating of the session
  1   2   3   4   5

ADDITIONAL COMMENTS:_____

Appendix H

Staff Development Follow-Up Questionnaire

By taking time to fill out this questionnaire honestly, you will help us to evaluate our progress toward district goals and plan more effective experiences for you.

1. On the final day of the Inservice Series on _____, how did you rate the series?

   Low   High
  1   2   3   4   5

2. In retrospect, do you feel you should have rated it:
    Lower Than I Did   Higher Than I Did   The Same
    Why? Please be specific_____

_____

(Examples: At the time I agreed with the majority of ideas presented, but... OR I wish I had been introduced to this earlier, because ... OR This topic has potential, but the training needs to be changed in the following way ... OR I thought I could use the suggestions, but... OR It seemed that I had always used the effective questioning techniques, but ...)

3. Have you tried to implement anything presented at these inservices? Please provide as complete a summary as possible. After each, please give a number indicating the success rate.

Will continue to use   Was O.K   Won't try again
  1   2   3   4   5
If you have not used any ideas presented at the inservice, please share your reasons_____

_____

4. To what extent have you discussed/compared with other teachers any of the techniques covered in the inservice?

At least once a week   Not at all
1   2   3   4   5
If yes, was this discussion helpful? _____

5. To what extent have you discussed/compared any of the techniques covered by the presenter with your school administrator(s)?
At least once a week   Not at all
1   2   3   4   5
If yes, was this discussion productive?_____

6. Do you feel a need for more information/direction?   Yes   No
If yes, in which areas? Check those which are appropriate.
_____ Implementation in the Classroom
_____ Ways of Assessing Success of the Techniques
_____ Review of Materials/Ideas Presented, as listed here
_____ Other_____

7. In which of the following formats would you like for information to be presented? Indicate your level of preference by placing a number in each blank.
Strongly prefer   O.K.   Will do   Maybe   Do not want
5   4   3   2   1
District Staff Development
___ inservice
___ reading/discussion groups
___ peer coaching
___ observation in other classrooms
___ other (describe) _____
District Inservices
___ 1 or 2 hours
___ 1/2 day
___ full day
___ multiple sessions of _____length
___ during school year, on Saturday
___ during summer, in ____June, or ____July, or ____ August
Credit Courses
___ during school year, in the evening

___ during school year, on Saturday
___ during the summer

8. Please list the goals you set for yourself at the end of the inservice.

_____

_____

9. Indicate the progress you have made toward these goals.

_____

_____

10. Indicate barriers you have encountered in attaining these goals._____